Roger S

The Corporate I

ethicability®

ETHICABILITY is a UK registered Trade Mark of Roger Steare Consulting Limited.

MORALDNA is an EU registered Trade Mark of Roger Steare Consulting Limited.

First published in the United Kingdom
First edition 2006
Second edition 2008
Third edition 2009
Fourth edition 2011
Fifth edition 2013
Fifth edition, paperback, 2019

ISBN 978-0-9935712-1-3

Edited by Jacky Fitt, Big Ideas Collective

Designed by Ned Hoste, 2h Design

Illustrations by Tim Bulmer

Proofreading by Alison Farrell

Indexing by Sarah Hilton

Printed by Beamreach Printing

For Dad

" 'Doing the right thing' makes sound sense for any business with long-lasting aspirations. But saying it and doing it are different things. Which is where *ethicability* comes in."
Mark Parsons, Deputy CEO, Barclays UK Retail & Business Bank

"Roger makes the compelling case for why doing the right thing is not a function of a good business, it **is** good business."
Joe Garner, Deputy CEO & Head of UK Retail, HSBC Bank plc

"Roger has had a significant influence on our efforts to continuously reinforce the concept of doing the right thing in all our business activities. His *ethicability* model provides a framework to transform difficult grey areas into a more simple, fundamental approach to making decisions we can be proud of."
Tom McCormick, Group Ethics & Compliance Officer, BP

"Developing the wisdom to know 'what is right' is a lot more difficult than most people think. Finding the courage to act on it is even harder. *ethicability* is a thoughtful and insightful guide with examples of many real world ethical dilemmas to help individuals ask the right questions and build the confidence to make decisions based on integrity and principles. Roger Steare's book will be a gem to companies and individuals wishing to develop a moral compass."
John Harker, Director of HR and Corporate Affairs, Citi EMEA

"When people ask me to define what it means to behave ethically, my response to them is that it is about 'doing the right thing.' At British Gas it is this behaviour that shapes our relationships with customers, our colleagues and society at large. In *ethicability* Roger Steare captures the essence of business integrity in a wonderfully practical and accessible way."
Anne Minto OBE, Group Director, Human Resources, Centrica plc

"It was not so very long ago that a person's honour was of such value that any questioning of it resulted in duels to the death or migration to the far colonies. Honour (read: ethical and moral fibre) really mattered. It seems that as society has become increasingly prescriptive about 'right and wrong', we have come to rely less on *ethicability* perhaps because personal judgement has been dulled by an increasingly regulated social environment. Roger's book explores this topic most absorbingly."
Michael Kirkwood CMG, Director, UKFI

"As institutional shareholders we need to remember that ultimately we don't invest in securities, we invest in people. For executives to act with responsibility and for boards to accept accountability, they can now decide what's right with *ethicability* – and this of course applies to us as investors."
Lindsay Tomlinson OBE, Chairman, National Association of Pension Funds

"Both in the long term and at the end of the day the returns of a pension fund investment portfolio are not only judged by the numbers. Every day, in front of the mirror, we have to pass another test; have we, to the best of our knowledge, 'done the right thing'? Here, Roger's book will be of much help to us in putting *ethicability* principles into practice in the jungle of unwritten and written rules and regulations in the financial markets."
Roderick Munsters, CEO, Robeco Groep N.V.

"Roger's work has helped our senior team engage with what it really means to operate in a principles-based way."
David Sims, CEO Global Life Emerging Markets, Zurich

"This book combines ethical theory, practical psychology and commercial examples to build a workable method for wise decision-making. I commend *ethicability* to those who want business with soul as well as profit."
Father Christopher Jamison OSB, author of Finding Happiness *and star of* BBC2's The Monastery

"Through *ethicability*, Roger has demonstrated that he has one of the most important traits of great thought leadership, the ability to make simple what others find complex. Politicians, business leaders, employees and people the world over will benefit."
Ali Gill, Organisational Psychologist, getfeedback.net and three times Olympian

"*ethicability* is wonderful. It's so honest and straightforward and a great balance of theory, reflection, understanding and practice. I particularly like the fact that it's very readily digestible, without a hint of dumbing-down the importance of the message. It's 100 % fit for purpose."
Carrie Bedingfield, OneFish TwoFish, B2B Marketing

"In our world today, not only do we see more law-breaking, but many people seem to have lost any sense of how to judge whether something is right or wrong. Not only does *ethicability* remind us how to decide what's right, it also reminds us why this is so important. I applaud and congratulate Roger Steare on his efforts and for the clarity of his guidance."
Chief Superintendent (Retired) David Seaborn Davies, former Head of Royal Protection, Metropoliltan Police Service

"It is time for each and every one of us to examine how our behaviour affects others. *ethicability* provides a valuable resource for businesses, authorities and individuals to reflect on what they do and then without hesitation have the courage to do what is RIGHT."
Gary Brown, founder of Knight School

"The array of choices in the twenty-first century business world and the speed with which they have to be made can be more bewildering than at any previous point in human history. *ethicability* will help you to discern what is right and what is wrong and will provide you with a vital tool for making those difficult choices."
John Pocock, Entrepreneur, and former CEO, Druid plc

"I enjoy working with Roger Steare because he is robust, principled, practical and good company. His book is the same – make the most of it."
Mark Goyder, Founder Director Tomorrow's Company

"Ethics is a word that people feel they should understand but mostly shy away from. Reading *ethicability* will bring this difficult word alive. The book is down to earth, readable yet comprehensive and widely sourced. It will also provide its reader with a practical tool to deal with the everyday dilemmas we all face in life. A tool that meets the author's aim 'to help us to decide what's right and then find the courage to do it' through learning, understanding and applying the meaning of RIGHT."
Philippa Foster Back OBE, Director, Institute of Business Ethics

"Dilemma: read or not read? Answer: read with gusto. The field of judgement and careful reasoning needed an accessible, credible and insightful guide. With *ethicability* Roger has delivered one."
Sebastian Bailey, The Mind Gym

Contents

"In the book of life,
the answers aren't in the back."

Charlie Brown

"Life is the sum of
 all your choices."

Albert Camus

Preface to the fifth edition

The first edition of ethicability in 2006 was the product of four years work with business leaders who want to do the right thing. Now, after 16 years working with new clients and many thousands of business executives, ethicability has evolved into a critical component of the "moral compass" that guides us both personally and collectively.

The questions that I ask people to ask and answer – both for themselves as individuals and for their businesses - are these:

1. Why do you exist? What is your purpose? How will you sustain it?

2. Who are you? What are your values? How do people describe your character?

3. How do you make difficult decisions in the moments that matter?

4. How do you act? What behaviour do people observe and tell stories about? Do your actions sustain your purpose?

These four sets of questions form a virtuous circle or moral compass with *ethicability* providing us with our standard of judgement or decision making framework.

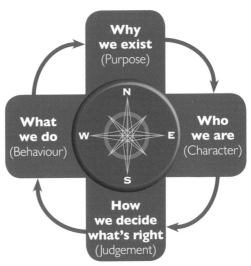

After asking and answering these questions, the responsibility of good business leaders is to lead by example, to "be the change you want to see" as Gandhi once said. We call this leadership action. But it's also partly to change what we might call the cultural enablers that support this moral eco-system. This begins with leaders creating a culture of psychological safety for their teams, so that honest, open debate is encouraged and everyone can speak truth to power.

Finally, I would like to thank all those clients, many of whom have become friends, for your feedback, love and support over the last 16 years. As we move into a period of environmental, social and economic meltdown, I do hope that *ethicability* will continue to help all of us stop and think about the decisions we make and find the courage to do what's right. I truly believe our civilization is on the edge of an abyss and we will all need to find the love, wisdom and courage to survive.

January 2019

Genesis

This book has been written to fill a void. How do we decide what's right and find the courage to do it?

We live in a world where we're constantly told what's right and we're losing the ability to work it out for ourselves. From parents to teachers, from preachers to the boss, we're told, "do this," "don't do that," "here's your bonus" or "you're fired." Yet most of us really don't like being told what's right. Surely we can be trusted to work it out for ourselves. But with everyone else telling us what to think and do, where can we learn how to do this? We can find thousands of books on how to be happy or how to be a success. We might even find ourselves looking at the philosophy section in a bookshop, but after flipping through books using words like "chrematistics," "epistemology" and "propositional calculus," we put them back on the shelf, having lost the will to live.

ethicability has been written to fill this void. Its purpose is to help you learn how to decide what's right and to find the courage to do it. It's not a textbook in philosophy, although its pragmatic approach does draw on established moral theories and social psychology. The author is not an academic, but business leaders, corporate learning professionals, business schools, universities and psychologists have acknowledged that ethicability works for real people facing real choices in the real world.

Whilst ethicability was initially created to respond to the challenges facing businesses, it became clear that these could not be addressed in isolation, nor could the approach itself have integrity unless it could be applied to dilemmas faced across the spectrum of our personal, public and professional lives. Ethicability has evolved and been tested with audiences as diverse as cynical investment bankers; general practitioners juggling Hippocratic duty with financial targets; and even married couples wondering whether it's right to stay together "for the sake of the kids." Ethicability won't tell you what's right, but it will help you reach a reasonable decision. It will then help you find the courage to do what's right, because you will have the confidence that you've made your decision with integrity. You will not only be able to justify your actions to others, but also to yourself. You may come to realise that doing the right thing is not always about success or happiness – it sometimes means that we have to make personal sacrifices and accept short-term setbacks as well as emotional or physical pain. Life isn't a playground.

Ethicability is about being good, doing right, and leaving the world a better place.

"I am always ready to learn, although I do not always like being taught."

Winston Churchill

Scene setting

Why are ethics important? Do they matter? Do we care about rising divorce rates, AIDS, street violence, alcohol, tobacco and drug abuse, terrorism, torture, environmental issues, corporate and political scandal? How do we decide what's right when it comes to abortion, euthanasia and stem-cell research? At work, do we put profit ahead of principle? In our personal lives, do we put things before people? Why do some of us ignore our next-door neighbours, yet feel compelled to donate to people facing disaster on the other side of the world? Why do we react so strongly to the threat of the terrorist, when more people are killed or injured in a week on our roads than murdered and maimed in a year by terrorist bombs?

These are vital questions. They are vital socially, politically, economically and spiritually. The media parades countless experts telling us what to think and do. Is the right-wing or left-wing politician right? Do we believe the policeman who says we need longer detention without charge, or the judge who says we ought to preserve our hard-won freedoms? Do we believe the oil company CEO or the ecologist? Do we listen to the preacher, the psychologist or the celebrity?

The challenge we face today is that the forces of industrialisation and democracy have created a world where the dominant ethos is to maximise personal economic happiness for the voting majority. Minority interests are then supposed to be protected by social legislation and personal conscience. Politicians say, "It's the economy, stupid,"[1] followed by the

"Did you ever stop to think, and forget to start again?"

Winnie the Pooh

"I'll keep it short and sweet – Family. Religion. Friendship. These are the three demons you must slay if you wish to succeed in business."

Montgomery Burns, *The Simpsons*, Twentieth Century Fox Film Corporation

apology that, "Something must be done," when something stupid is done. Philosophers have described this ethos as "weak rule utilitarianism,"[2] which means that what's right is whatever benefits the greatest number but with some safeguards called laws, which we'll break when the end justifies the means.

In business, executives are expected to ask and answer two questions when making decisions: "Is it profitable?" and "Is it legal?" Milton Friedman has argued strongly that, "There is one and only one social responsibility of business – to use its resources and engage in activities designed to increase its profits, so long as it stays within the rules of the game."[3] that is, the law. Armies of accountants, auditors and lawyers have been hired and deployed to build businesses which are, indeed, both profitable and legal. But few in business, the public sector or even society in general ask or answer a third and most important question: "Is it right?"

So why should we ask the question, "Is it right?" The answer can be clearly illustrated with reference to a story in the British press in September 2005.[4] Several major British retailers were selling "sexy" clothes and underwear for girls as young as six. This is clearly profitable and yes, it's legal. But is it right? For health campaigners, the answer was an emphatic,

"No, it is not right," and the clothing ranges were withdrawn by two of the stores named. This begs the question, did the store buyers think this was right in the first place, or did they just fail to ask themselves this question? In 2011 this issue remains contentious as pressure by the UK online forum Mumsnet, through their *Let Girls be Girls* campaign, and broadcaster Channel 4's programme *Stop Pimping Our Kids*[5] continues to be directed towards certain high street retailers who still fail to acknowledge anything unethical about aspects of their children's clothing lines.

The sexualisation of children is one area where business can be wrong whilst still acting lawfully and making profits, but there are many other areas which regularly make the headlines. Consumers are victims of legal, but extortionate business activities; employees are at risk of workplace exploitation, discrimination and abuse; and let's not forget the environmental impact of "legal" levels of pollutants, or the social impact of legalised narcotics, such as tobacco and alcohol.

In sum, the ethical challenges we face today have never been greater. The prospect of a nuclear holocaust may have receded, but the fallout we face today from our mindlessness about these issues is just as dangerous as any weapon of mass destruction.

Summary

Standards of living are up, but standards for living are down. Our obsessive focus on economic growth has been described as "the philosophy of the cancer cell" and we've found a lump. Will we continue to put things before people, or will we put principles before profits? Do we mis-sell a pension or miss this month's target? Do we buy fruit out of season, or do we consider carbon emissions? Do we do what's legal or do what's right – and how do we decide?

"Growth for the sake of growth is the philosophy of the cancer cell."

Edward Abbey

How to use this book

Ethicability evolved within the demanding environment of corporate training, where time is money. Its original challenge was to enable delegates in just two hours:

- to understand moral philosophy, neurophilosophy and moral psychology;

- to learn the ethicability decision-making framework; and

- to practise using ethicability with real and relevant scenarios

This book offers you these same learning opportunities. The learning model is based on Socrates's insight that, "I cannot teach anyone anything; I can only make them think." So this book will present you with a number of facts, insights and propositions that are designed to help you think for yourself.

The design, layout and typography are designed to work both for speed readers and for those with more time. Each section of the book contains an executive summary and some quotes, references or other visuals supporting more conventional text. It can be read in summary, re-read in detail, and used as a reference. The ethicability framework is also on a card attached to the inside of the book cover for you to keep handy in your wallet or purse.

This book is designed as a complete learning resource for the individual. However, at the organisational level it is highly recommended that the book is used to support an interactive workshop programme with specific, relevant dilemmas and scenarios. Details of these services are listed in the closing pages.

I hope you find this book as thought-provoking to read as it was for me to write. Ultimately, I hope you will find it helps you to lead a better life – a good life.

A morning's work for the speed reader

"You can't go around building a better world for people. Only people can build a better world for people. Otherwise it's just a cage."

Terry Pratchett, *Witches Abroad*

What is ethics?

What is ethics?

The first part of this book explores what we mean by "ethics." We begin by exploring three dominant moral philosophies, each of which plays a vital part in helping us to decide what's right. We will also look at what we mean by the word "integrity." Then it's important to understand why we do what's right or wrong at the psychological level. That is, why do good people do bad things? We will look at ethics as the way we resolve conflicts of desire, conflicts of interest and conflicts of principle. Finally, we will begin to look at how we apply ethics in the real world – at the personal level, as professionals in business and work, in bioethics and environmental issues, and finally, in law enforcement and the use of military force.

Before we begin, let's look at each of the following ethical scenarios. With each I have suggested an ethical course of action, but which of the reasons stated would you give for doing the right thing? Please be honest – all the answers are "right" in their own way.

1. You try to withdraw £100 from a cash machine, but instead it dispenses £200, because it's been incorrectly stacked with £20 notes instead of £10 notes. You decide to return the extra cash that isn't yours because:
    a. **I might get found out and prosecuted for theft.**
    b. **It wouldn't be fair to the bank's shareholders.**
    c. **It is simply wrong not to return someone else's property.**

2. You have decided to apply for a new job, but you do not have quite enough experience in one key area. However, you decide not to exaggerate your experience because:
    a. **It would be fraud and I could be . red if found out later.**
    b. **If everyone lied, who could we trust?**
    c. **Honesty is an important principle for me.**

3. You have been asked to take an "integrity test." You decide to answer truthfully because:

   a. The rm would expect me to take this seriously and comply.
   b. It's the fair thing to do for everyone involved.
   c. I'd rather face up to my weaknesses.

4. After nine months out of work, you get a great new job. However, one day your boss verbally abuses a young female colleague, reducing her to tears. You decide to act because:

   a. There are clear HR procedures to deal with this situation.
   b. Others might suffer if I don't take action.
   c. I'd rather risk my job than allow this kind of behaviour.

5. Your boss is a single-parent mother with two difficult children. She calls in sick and says she will be off work for a week, but the next day you see her coming out of the local cinema with her screaming children. You decide you have to act because:

   a. Lying about sick leave is fraud.
   b. I have the interests of all employees to consider.
   c. Trust is vital to working relationships.

Please note how many times you answered a, b or c. Each answer represents one of the three main moral philosophies that guide our sense of what's right, which we will call:

   a. Ethic of Obedience

   b. Ethic of Care

   c. Ethic of Reason

Three moral consciences

The Oxford Dictionary of English[6] defines ethics as, "moral principles that govern a person's behaviour," and morals as, "principles of right and wrong behaviour." Moral also means to be, "concerned with, based on, or adhering to the code of behaviour that is considered right or acceptable in a particular society rather than legal rights and duties." With these definitions, we can now describe the three dominant philosophies in our world today. The Ethic of Obedience is defined by our "legal rights and duties"; the Ethic of Care focuses on what "is considered right or acceptable in a particular society" based on empathic "moral principles" such as love and humility; and the Ethic of Reason is defined by those rational principles such as wisdom and self-control that help us to make a thoughtful decision about what's right. These definitions help us to understand that ethics is about both principles as well as rules. However, our developing understanding of how our brains function also means we must consider how we, as human beings, think and feel when we make difficult decisions. We are not robots. We empathise as well as rationalise when we make tough ethical decisions.

Remember our earlier cash machine example? If we give the money back because it's illegal to keep it, it is our Ethic of Obedience that is driving our decision and behaviour. If we give the money back because it belongs to other people, our Ethic of Care helps us to consider how others will feel if we take their money. Finally, if we give the money back because we stop and think about what we're doing and exercise self-control over our greed, this is our Ethic of Reason.

For each ethical conscience we will look at: a brief description of how it helps us to decide what's right; a summary of its history and influence; some insights on moral maturity and gender difference; and how we tend to prefer using different consciences with different groups of people and in different circumstances. Additionally, Table 1 (see page 37) provides a detailed comparison of these three philosophies.

"He's the one who stole the car, evaded arrest when cornered then kicked the policeman and according to his moralDNA he couldn't care less!"

Tim Bulmer

Ethic of Obedience

The Ethic of Obedience is the moral theory of "rights and duties," sometimes described by philosophers as "deontology" from the Greek "deon," meaning obligation. These rights and duties can be considered as "universal," for example Article 3 of the United Nations Universal Declaration of Human Rights states that "Everyone has the right to life, liberty and security of person." Rights and duties can also be legal – for example a landlord may have a legal right to evict tenants if they won't pay the agreed rent.

The Ethic of Obedience does not invite us to think about what's right or wrong, it tells us. It is wrong to steal someone else's property because there are laws against theft. We do not drink and drive because we have a duty to respect traffic laws. We pay our taxes because we have a legal duty to do so.

At their best, rules based on rights and duties are helpful for two reasons. Firstly, if we think of them as "applied principles," they help us to agree what is fair, particularly in complex situations. For example, if we didn't have taxation, how would we raise the money we need to build public schools, hospitals or roads? Secondly, they help us to deal with people in our society who care less about others or who have no conscience at all, such as sociopaths. If people are unable to act from moral principles or consider the consequences of their actions, then they need to be told what's right. Modern icons for the Ethic of Obedience include speed cameras and the seemingly ever increasing volume of health and safety regulations, governing those of us deemed too incapable, or more possibly too lazy, to adopt rational and empathic adult behaviour.

*"The more corrupt the state,
the greater the number of laws."*

Tacitus

"Integrity has no need of rules."

Albert Camus

At their worst, rules, laws, regulations and red tape have a tendency to multiply, because they remove our responsibility for deciding what's right. We can see this most clearly in corporate and political scandals. Since 2000, dozens of organisations, such as Enron, WorldCom, Parmalat and, more recently, Lehman Brothers, together with scores of banks and other financial service businesses, have been damaged by the unethical behaviour of a minority of directors and employees. Billions of dollars have been lost by shareholders and thousands of jobs have been destroyed. Governments have responded with even more rules and regulations, but haven't considered that it was a greed and fear-driven "obedience" culture that failed in the first place. In his book *The Corporation*,[7] Joel Bakan makes a powerful argument that…

"…the corporation's legally defined mandate is to pursue relentlessly and without exception its own economic self-interest, regardless of the harmful consequences it might cause to others… The corporation's unbridled self-interest victimizes individuals, society, and, when it goes awry, even shareholders and can cause corporations to self-destruct."

The corporation is simply a legal fiction. It is not "human" and has no conscience of its own. Therefore we need to ask ourselves if more rules will work any better. Can we imagine a world where we can write enough rules to cover every situation? Lawyers and accountants may be trying, but it's hard to imagine a world where this is either likely or desirable.

Human society has had rules, laws and taboos for thousands of years. The history of civilization has been fundamentally shaped by the impact of formal legal systems specifying legal rights and duties dating back more than 4,000 years to the Code of Hammurabi in ancient Mesopotamia, to Roman law in the fifth century BC, and to the Magna Carta in the thirteenth century. However, deontology has a relatively recent history as a moral framework. Immanuel Kant (1724 – 1804) argued against emerging utilitarianism by saying that if we believe in rights and duties, ends can never justify means. Kant's "categorical imperative" clearly states, for example, that we have a universal duty or obligation always to keep promises, irrespective of the consequences. However, the modern philosopher John Rawls has refined deontology into a theory of justice as "fairness," rather than the blunt categorical imperative of Kant. Rawls argued that "justice as fairness" has two principles. The first and overriding principle is that individual liberties, for example the right to freedom of speech, must be upheld. The second is that the welfare of the least advantaged members of society must be raised: the Ethic of Obedience meets the Ethic of Care.

Lawrence Kohlberg (1928 – 87) was a psychologist and professor of education at Harvard University. He developed an influential theory of moral development based on empirical research that analysed the way subjects decided whether it was right for a man to steal a drug in order to save the life of his dying wife.[8] He identified six stages of moral development that we begin as young children when we obey rules for reward or fear of punishment.

In terms of moral maturity, Kohlberg places our Ethic of Obedience at the beginning of his theory, from Stage 1 in early childhood, which he described as "obedience and punishment orientation," to Stage 3 in adolescence, described as "interpersonal accord and conformity." More simply, moral infants obey rules for reward or fear of punishment. So, ask yourself whether we live and work in a world which treats us as moral grown-ups or as frightened moral infants? Which would be the better place to live?

Summary

The Ethic of Obedience tells us what's right: "do not think, just obey". This moral perspective helps when we can't always agree what's right, or when some people just don't seem to have a conscience at all, or if they do, when they choose to ignore it. However, too many rules tend to make us lazy in taking responsibility for thinking about what's right and we can never write enough rules to cover every situation. It's a useful framework for everyday living and helps us interact safely with people we've never met before. We can trust a friend, but we need the assurance of rules and contractual rights and duties when buying something from a stranger on the Internet.

Ends Justify means?

"The things that will destroy America are prosperity-at-any-price, peace-at-any-price, safety-first instead of duty-first, the love of soft living, and the get-rich-quick theory of life."

President "Teddy" Roosevelt

Ethic of Care

The Ethic of Care is closest to the philosophy of "consequentialism" or "utilitarianism". Utility, in this case, means that what is right is what benefits the greatest number of people. We may also look at the consequences of our actions and consider who might benefit or be harmed by a course of action. For example, we might decide to report a bully at work because we don't want others to suffer. In historical terms, the Ethic of Care as a concept would certainly have been understood by philosophers such as Thomas Hobbes, Adam Smith and Jean-Jacques Rousseau, who all correctly understood that human prosperity is based on co-operation and the concept of the "social contract," rather than individualism, selfish competition and the "law of the jungle." To quote Hobbes, without co-operation and empathy, life would be "solitary, poor, nasty, brutish and short."[9]

In Kohlberg's Theory of Moral Development, the Ethic of Care is found in adolescence at Level 4, which Kohlberg described as, "authority and social-order maintaining orientation," and in early adulthood at Level 5, described as, "social contract orientation." In other words, if we consider the consequences of our actions on others, then we are well on the way to becoming moral grown-ups.

Carol Gilligan (1936 –), a student of Kohlberg's, was critical of his theory because most of the subjects were men and she believed that women can think differently about morals. Gilligan's own research[10] analysed the moral choices made by women when faced by an abortion dilemma. It is Gilligan's theories, with their focus on community and relationships, which are most consistent with the Ethic of Care. It is empathy that provides the moral foundation for our relationships with family, friends and neighbours; and at work with our customers and colleagues.

The Ethic of Care is also about the "feeling" moral values or principles of love, fairness and humility. With these values, the Ethic of Care helps us to build and maintain *social* integrity.

More recent discoveries in neuroscience have added further to the evidence that the Ethic of Care is vital to human well-being and doing the right thing. We will touch on this again later in the book.

Summary

The Ethic of Care helps us to decide what's right by considering the consequences, both good and bad, of our actions on others. Centred on our feelings of love, fairness and empathy, the Ethic of Care is a crucial part of our moral character and helps us to decide what's right in both our working, as well as personal relationships.

Ethic of Reason

Philosophers will understand some of what we mean by the Ethic of Reason as "virtue ethics." Virtues, principles or values, such as wisdom and self-control, define our character or who we are. To put it another way, it's about how we use our "thinking" brain, or neocortex, to control our more primitive drives. We do what's right because it's the wise or moderate thing to do. Our behaviour is a function not just of our empathic emotions and the Ethic of Care, it's also about the rational decisions we make. Our goal in life is not pleasure or even happiness; our goal is to lead a good life. The thinking principles or values we believe in define our personal integrity.

Although it's a powerful philosophy, the Ethic of Reason presents us with some difficulties. The first challenge we face with these "thinking" moral principles is that they sometimes conflict; for example, "truth" often conflicts with "loyalty." For instance, do we report a close colleague who is discussing confidential matters with a competitor? Principles are also a guide to action, and may not be very specific. They can, therefore, be open to interpretation, argument and disagreement. But the biggest challenge with rational principles is that doing what's right will often demand great courage – for example, when we have to admit we've done something wrong.

The Greek philosopher Aristotle (384 – 322 BC) is recognised as the founder of this school of ethics and his influence is pervasive; for example, the medieval philosopher St. Thomas Aquinas used many of Aristotle's insights to support Catholic theology. Whilst his teachings fell out of favour as Western societies urbanised and industrialised, virtue ethics is now enjoying a renaissance amongst contemporary philosophers such as Alasdair MacIntyre.[11]

The Ethic of Reason is equivalent to Kohlberg's sixth and final stage, which he described as the "stage of universal principles." In other words, moral grown-ups will exercise the Ethic of Reason when deciding what's right. Our own research into MoralDNA is also consistent with Kohlberg's theory as it clearly shows the Ethic of Reason significantly increasing with age, as the Ethic of Obedience declines. The implications of this inverse correlation will be examined in more detail later in the book.

Summary

The Ethic of Reason helps us to decide what's right by thinking though our actions and making rational choices. It also helps us to exercise self-control and restraint. Whilst the Ethic of Care appears to be a constant throughout our lives, the Ethic of Reason develops and grows, as we gain experience in making good (and not so good) decisions.

"It's not hard to make decisions when you know what your values are."

Roy Disney

Summary

Ethics is defined as moral values that guide our behaviour, together with legal rights and duties that are acceptable in a particular society. We can identify three dominant philosophies in ethics: the Ethic of Obedience, the Ethic of Care and the Ethic of Reason.

Table 1 compares these moral philosophies.

Whilst we can clearly see the differences in these philosophies, we should also see the connections between them. With the Ethic of Obedience, we can think of rules as moral values we have applied within a specific context. When we consider others in terms of the Ethic of Care, we are *feeling* the values of love and humility. When we consider the values of wisdom and self-control, we are *thinking* of the Ethic of Reason.

With real dilemmas facing real people in real life, ethicability uses each of these moral frameworks to help us decide what's right. In fact, the key to ethicability is the following set of questions, which we can remember as the mnemonic "RIGHT". We need to ask:

- What are the **Rules**?
- Are we acting with **Integrity**?
- Who is this **Good** for?
- Who could we **Harm**?
- What's the **Truth**?

The RIGHT questions are the core of the ethicability framework and can be used alone if you need to make a quick decision as well as the RIGHT decision.

Table 1. Ethical Philosophies Compared

	Ethic of Obedience	Ethic of Care	Ethic of Reason
Philosophers call it…	deontology	utilitarianism	virtue ethics
What's right is…	our compliance with what's legal; our legal rights and duties	our empathic sense of what benefits most people and harms the least	our rational judgement based on wisdom and self-control
We act with…	fear	empathy	reason
As seen mostly within…	schools, bureaucracies and big business	family, friendship, neighbourhood and SMEs	universities, bureaucracies and big business
The weaknesses are…	we stop thinking for ourselves; too many rules create more rule-breaking; too many rules stifle creativity	minorities are marginalised; the end justifies the means; pleasure preferred over what's good	purely rational decisions will be flawed if we do not have all the information we need for this calculus

"One of the reasons we have so much regulation is because we cannot rely on people stopping to think about what's right"

Michael Kirkwood [12]

Integrity
– it's a matter of principle

Having explored three ethical philosophies, we now need to consider the concept of integrity as a word which can develop our understanding of what is right. The word integrity is currently found in more than 185 million web pages.[13] It is a word we use to describe reputation, honesty and trustworthiness. Yet integrity is much more than that. In our paper "Integrity in Practice" co-written with Abbot Christopher Jamison in 2003, we described integrity as "those shared values, attitudes and behaviours that help us to act correctly in our lives at home at work and in society."[14] In other words, integrity is the principle that defines all our other principles. We have integrity if we live our lives according to principles. If, however, we act against those principles, then we lose our integrity. We call this hypocrisy. If we doubt the integrity of others without just cause, we call this cynicism.

Integrity has meaning both at the personal and at the social level. Our *personal* integrity is another way of looking at our Ethic of Reason. We have personal integrity when we are able to exercise reason and self-control over our more primitive wants. Our *social* integrity relates to our Ethic of Care. If we care about others, this empathy is how we build the social integrity of family, friendship, neighbourhood and workplace.

But integrity also means a sense of what is right, in that we choose to obey the law, provided laws are democratic and just. In this sense we can also invoke the Ethic of Obedience. Integrity helps us to incorporate the notion of rights and duties, which we define as the principle of justice or fairness. For example, whilst most of us dislike paying taxes, it is the fairest way we can contribute to the public good. We only have a right to enjoy the protection of the police, for example, when we fulfil our duty and pay our fair share of taxes. Tax avoidance is legal, but is it right?

In order to understand how integrity helps us to decide what's right, we therefore need to explore the key principles which together define our integrity. There are four "cardinal" virtues we have inherited from the ancient Greek philosophers. These are Prudence, Justice, Fortitude and Temperance, which we will call Wisdom, Fairness, Courage and Self-Control. There are three further "theological" virtues that were defined by the mediaeval Christian church and that are also found in every other major religion. These are Faith (which we will call Trust), Hope and Love. To these, we can add three others that resonate with people today. These are Honesty, Humility and Excellence.

Wisdom
"Wisdom is the supreme part of happiness." Sophocles

Fairness
"Man is a rational animal, endowed by nature with rights and with an innate sense of justice." Thomas Jefferson

Courage
"It is curious that physical courage should be so common in the world and moral courage so rare." Mark Twain

Self-Control
"Patience is the companion of wisdom." St. Augustine

Trust
"It is better to suffer wrong than to do it, and happier to be some times cheated than not to trust." Dr. Samuel Johnson

Hope
"Once you choose hope, anything's possible." Christopher Reeve ("Superman")

Love
"Whatever our souls are made of, his and mine are the same." Emily Brontë

Honesty
"Be honest to those who are honest, and be also honest to those who are not honest. Thus honesty is attained." Lao Tzu

Humility
"Blushing is the colour of virtue." Diogenes

Excellence
"We are what we repeatedly do. Excellence then, is not an act, but a habit." Aristotle

Let's begin by looking at each of these principles, what they mean, the opposite vice and the excess – too much of a good thing! After all, ancient Greek philosophers said that too much of a virtue is a vice.

How important are each of these principles for you at home, at work and with family and friends? Are there any differences in their importance depending on where you are and who you're with? What do you most admire in others? Do your friends have these qualities? Which virtues, vices and excesses do you see at work? What about in society? We will look at how real people actually do measure up to these principles when we consider integrity testing a little later.

Table 2. Virtues, vices and excesses

Moral Value	Which means...	Vice	Excess
Wisdom	Prudence, caution, good sense, mindfulness	Recklessness	Procrastination
Fairness	Justice, impartiality, rights and duties	Injustice, prejudice	Rigidity, callousness
Courage	Stamina, guts, grit, fortitude, determination	Fear, laziness	Stubbornness
Self-control	Patience, self-discipline, restraint, temperance	Greed, impatience, violence, aggression	Self-obsession
Trust	Loyalty, faith commitment, reliance	Cynicism, betrayal	Naivety
Hope	Optimism, cheerfulness, confidence	Despair, misery	Fantasy, delusion
Love	Compassion, kindness, generosity, altruism	Fear, hate	Obsession, infatuation
Honesty	Openness, truthfulness, transparency	Deceit, denial, dishonesty	Hurtful, brutal
Humility	Modesty, diffidence	Arrogance, egotistical	False modesty, hypocrisy
Excellence	Quality, merit, doing the best we can	Mediocrity, failure	Perfectionism

"Integrity is the only thing between me and oblivion."

Michael Kirkwood

Summary

Integrity is the sum of all those principles that guide the way we live and behave with others. If we choose the right principles, we can draw on what's best in each of our moral traditions. Fairness helps us to respect rights and duties, whilst kindness, patience and trust help us make the world a better place. After all, who can argue with a life guided by wisdom, fairness, courage, patience, trust, optimism, generosity, honesty, excellence and respect?

"Integrity is doing the right thing. Knowing that nobody's going to know whether you did it or not."

Oprah Winfrey

Psychology

Having explored three moral consciences, we will now look at several psychological theories, which help us understand our behaviour, moral or otherwise. Psychology is a relatively recent scientific discipline, dating from 1879 when Wilhelm Wundt established the first dedicated psychology laboratory in Leipzig. However, philosophers have been interested in how our brain works for millennia, although only at a theoretical level. In fact, until the late 19th century, psychology was viewed as a branch of philosophy. Today, both moral psychology and neuroscience are helping us understand more about human morality. In this chapter, we will look at the emerging science of happiness; how our behaviour is connected to moral maturity; how our brains make decisions; how obedience to authority can explain why good people sometimes do bad things; and how integrity testing can help us develop awareness of our moral strengths and weaknesses – what we call "MoralDNA".

"Happiness is not best achieved by those who seek it directly."

Bertrand Russell

The science of happiness

At the biological level, we feel happy because of the effect of the neurotransmitter dopamine on the pleasure centres of the brain, known as mu-opioid receptors. In other words, we feel happy when a pleasure stimulant, such as a favourite food, creates a release of dopamine. Natural "highs" can result from activities such as physical intimacy or listening to music. We can also feel pleasure by taking drugs, such as morphine, which release artificial opiates into our bodies.

For most of us, most of the time, there's nothing wrong with the happiness we enjoy from a good meal or an intimate moment. In fact, if we didn't experience these pleasures, we would forget to eat or to make babies and the next thing we'd know, goodbye humanity! The problem we face is that our physical brains are still hard-wired to survive in a hostile world where the basics for life were scarce. When we see things that help us survive, we want to stockpile them, which might mean we overindulge in food or drink or we accumulate physical wealth far in excess of our needs. The reality for those of us who live in the developed world is that we have succeeded in creating environments where the risk of starvation homelessness or violence is relatively low, but we find it really difficult to switch off the primitive programming which compels us to want more than we need.

The psychologist Steven Reiss has referred to this kind of happiness as "feel-good" happiness. In his research, which is based on surveys completed by thousands of people across the social, economic and political spectrum,[15] he found that the problem with feel-good happiness is that it is subject to the law of diminishing returns. For example, when we pass a driving test and get our first car worth £500, the thrill is huge. Fast forward 10 years and we're buying our first luxury car that costs £50,000, but is the thrill as intense? Reiss's findings are also supported by the latest research collated by economist Richard Layard at the London School of Economics:[16] we each only need to earn the average national salary to meet our basic needs. Beyond this, happiness does not increase.

Steven Reiss also described a second kind of happiness in his research. He called this "value-based" happiness.

"Value-based happiness is the great equalizer in life. You can find value-based happiness if you are rich or poor, smart or mentally challenged, athletic or clumsy, popular or socially awkward. Wealthy people are not necessarily happy, and poor people are not necessarily unhappy. Values, not pleasure, are what bring true happiness, and everybody has the potential to live in accordance with their values."

Could it be that this "value-based" happiness might help us explain why good parents make sacrifices for their children; why friends will accept an inconvenience to help us out; or why we're prepared to support others less fortunate than ourselves?

"But what is happiness except the simple harmony between a man and the life he leads?"

Albert Camus

"*Father Crowley:*

'Gabrielle, you know, we are all responsible for the choices we make. Don't you want to be a good person?'

Gabrielle

'What I want is to be happy.'

Father Crowley:

'That's the answer of a selfish child.'"

Desperate Housewives, Series 1, Episode 8 Guilty, Touchstone Television, abc inc.

Summary

Philosophers, such as Aristotle, have spoken of a life lived in the pursuit of value-based happiness as "the good life." If we accept that the good life, a truly happy life, is lived according to a set of values rather than the value of our assets, then we need to decide whether an ethos that seeks to maximise economic well-being for the voting majority is the best we can do? Is it time for us to grow up not just as moral adults but as a mature, moral society? Is too much dopamine making us morally dumb and dumber?

"Games People Play"

In 1964, the American psychiatrist Eric Berne published a book called *Games People Play: The Psychology of Human Relationships*.[17] In the book, Berne mapped adult behaviour into three states: Parent, Adult and Child. He then identified the communication or role-play that occurred as adults interacted whilst playing these different roles. This technique is commonly referred to as Transactional Analysis or TA. Here are some simple interactions[18] we might find in the workplace:

Phil: "Have you been able to finish that report yet, Sophie?"
(Adult-to-Adult)

Sophie: "Yes, I'll send it to you now."
(Adult-to-Adult)

Phil: "Now we've finished, why don't we go out for a coffee?"
(Child-to-Child)

Sophie: "Yes, that would be great!"
(Child-to-Child)

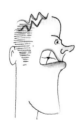

Phil: "I'm still waiting for that report, Sophie. Why isn't it ready yet?"
(Parent-to-Child)

Sophie: "Because *some* people keep interrupting and hassling me."
(Child-to-Parent)

The goal of TA is that we should live our lives according to our own values and principles, rather than those learned from or imposed by our parents or by those acting in loco parentis. TA is used to help people gain freedom from any unhelpful passive behaviours learned as a child, to gain autonomy as adults, and to learn how to resolve problems rather than react to them – or avoid them!

So how does looking at the games people play help us to decide what's right and find the courage to do it? Can we map Child, Parent and Adult behaviour into the Ethic of Obedience, the Ethic of Care and the Ethic of Reason? I believe we can. We can describe the Ethic of Care and the Ethic of Reason as Adult-to-Adult behaviour. Moral grown-ups will transact as adults, one with another. We will have the courage to face up to dilemmas and resolve them empathically and fairly. An example of this is the way that many businesses facing financial difficulty will honestly negotiate pay-cuts and shorter working hours with employees rather than the destructive Parent-to-Child transaction of forced redundancies.

We can also make some connections between the absence of the Ethic of Reason and Child-to-Child transactions. If we all behave as children who lack wisdom and self-control, then we run the risk of pursuing a shallow life devoted solely to fun and feel-good happiness. For example, should we be asking ourselves whether it is right to spend money on cosmetic surgery when millions are dying for lack of any basic healthcare?

We can describe the Ethic of Obedience in terms of Parent-to-Child and Child-t o-Parent transactions. If a few adults in authority behave as parents, we are likely to react as children and comply resentfully with the letter of the law, predictably seeking ever more devious ways to do what we want. Berne described the Parent-to-Child and Child-to-Parent transaction as a vicious circle. We can see this clearly in the way governments repeatedly try and fail to regulate corporate (and social) behaviour, particularly in the US. As we have already stated, executives at Enron, WorldCom, Parmalat and Lehman Brothers broke existing rules. Since then we have seen a huge increase in the burden of rules-based regulation. A typical corporation in a regulated industry such as banking, pharmaceuticals, energy and defence, has to comply with literally tens of thousands of rules, laws and regulation. Yet the continuing series of corporate scandals demonstrates the fundamental ineffectiveness of this approach. The alternative to this expanding plethora of regulation is to live the moral values we've discussed earlier. Here we have just ten moral values that have been effective in guiding our behaviour for millennia. As Albert Camus once wrote, "Integrity has no need of rules."

Parmalat broke existing rules. Since then we have seen a huge increase in the burden of regulation, particularly with the Sarbanes–Oxley Act of 2002. Regrettably we have also seen a series of new investigations at AIG, Bristol Myers-Squibb, Hollinger International and Sony BMG Entertainment.

Summary

Transactional Analysis provides us with a useful framework for understanding how we decide what's right. Do we act as a Parent and treat another adult like a Child? Do we act as a Child and view life as a playground? Or do we act as Adults, as moral grown-ups who take responsibility for their actions? What kind of behaviour do we believe is most likely to help us make the right decision?

"Growing old is mandatory; growing up is optional."

Chili Davis

Game theory, fairness and justice

How does our brain make decisions? As human beings, we like to think that we are rational creatures seeking a higher purpose in life than mere existence. In part, this is true. However, we must also recognise that our physical brains still contain more basic components which remain powerful drivers of thought, feelings and behaviour. The "reptilian complex" within our brain controls our basic biological functions like heartbeat, breathing, appetite and desire. This is the part that keeps us alive for example, by instantly reacting to threats – if we touch something hot, we will immediately pull our hand away. Next is our mammalian limbic system that controls positive emotions such as love, empathy and kindness. This part we share with animals like "man's best friend", the dog. The third part is the highly developed grey-matter neocortex, particularly the frontal lobe, where we process abstract thought and reason.

When we make decisions, each of these parts of our brain interacts. We can learn to control most of our basic instincts, most of the time. It's called civilisation. However, we are not computers that will respond precisely to programming rules. Take racism for example. Harvard social ethicist Mahzarin Banaji has conducted experiments using MRI brain scans.[19] These have shown that when we see a human being with a different skin colour, a part of our primitive brain (the amygdala) immediately reacts to the differences we see. Our neocortex may stop us from making a racist remark or worse, but whoever we are, this primitive reaction invariably occurs. No amount of diversity "training" will stop these primitive reactions, but we can learn to control them.

Let's now look at some research which demonstrates more clearly how our moral sense of fairness for example, is not simply a matter of rational calculus, it is also about our empathy. The "Ultimatum Game"[20] is one of the most popular experiments in behavioural economics. It has been extensively researched and analysed over the last 20 years and across different cultures from the US to Mongolia. There are two players in the game. The first player is given a sum of money, for example, $100, and has to offer the second player a proportion of this money, which the second player can accept or reject. Both players know how much is on the table. They know that if the second player accepts the offer, they both get to keep their respective shares; but that if the second player rejects the offer, they both lose everything – that's the ultimatum.

Game theory and the principle of utility in economics predict that a rational second player would accept any offer made by the first, even if it was $1. Any offer is better than nothing. However, in experiments across different cultures, including those where $100 represents over a week's average wage, most players reject offers below $20. The only group who consistently accepted lesser amounts were economics undergraduates! There are many complex theories proposed that might explain why most people would reject a low offer, but for many of the people I work with, the explanation is simple. We would rather lose the chance to benefit financially than see an injustice rewarded. For many people, fairness would mean a 50/50 split, but for others fairness means what is acceptable. Some researchers[21] have scanned the brain activity of second players immediately after a derisory offer has been made, with little higher brain activity in evidence, but much more in the primitive limbic system. Could this be rage and revenge?

What conclusions might we draw from these experiments? The first is to recognise the part that emotions play in the way we sense right and wrong. Does an emotional response to injustice mean that we are reacting purely from a selfish perspective, or have we also developed a form of social programming which means we want to punish unfair behaviour for the sake of others? At the philosophical level, we could argue that fairness is not something we can calculate arbitrarily, but is something we can create or not within a human interaction or relationship. We could call this a "shared value". We can also describe love, trust and hope as shared values.

Summary

Our brains do not function simply as rational computers. Our primitive survival instincts generate the fear and greed that are the primary drivers for doing the wrong thing. This is why we need an Ethic of Obedience. But ultimately it is the combination of our empathic and rational brains that enable us to be both mindful of others and thoughtful about our actions. It's about our shared values and our relationships. It's about our Ethic of Care and our Ethic of Reason. We can even see these philosophies at work, lighting up the human brain during MRI scans.

"Our lives are a constant dance between duty and desire."

Meera Syal

Conformity theory

Stanley Milgram, a psychologist at Yale University, conducted an experiment called a "Study of Obedience."[22] Milgram invited a cross-section of 40 ordinary American citizens to participate in what he described as a "Study of Memory," and those participants were joined by a number of actors masquerading as fellow participants. In the experiment, they were asked to work in pairs. One person (always the ordinary citizen) was asked to play the role of teacher and apply a fictitious and increasing electric shock whenever the pupil (always the actor, who sat in a room next door) answered a memory question incorrectly. As the voltages "increased," the actor would be prompted to scream or bang on the wall and shout for the pain to stop. If the teacher hesitated or questioned the safety of the experiment, they would be reassured that they would not be held personally responsible for any injury and were firmly told to continue. The final voltage to be applied was a potentially lethal 450 volts. No less than 65 % of these ordinary, law-abiding citizens did what they were told to do and applied a shock of 450 volts. They were each paid $4.50 for their time. Milgram later wrote:

> "The legal and philosophic aspects of obedience are of enormous import, but they say very little about how most people behave in concrete situations. I set up a simple experiment at Yale University to test how much pain an ordinary citizen would inflict on another person simply because he was ordered to by an experimental scientist. Stark authority was pitted against the subjects' strongest moral imperatives against hurting others, and, with the subjects' ears ringing with the screams of the victims, authority won more often than not. The extreme willingness of adults to go to almost any lengths on the command of an authority constitutes the chief finding of the study and the fact most urgently demanding explanation."[23]

"All it takes for evil to flourish is for good men to do nothing."

Edmund Burke

Milgram's experiment was repeated by other psychologists across different cultures with remarkably little variation. Milgram's biographer, Thomas Blass, collated all the results of these experiments and demonstrated that between 61 % and 66 % of people were prepared to inflict potentially fatal voltages on fellow human beings when told to do so.[24] Others have since discussed this phenomenon in the context of the My Lai massacre in Vietnam and prisoner abuse at Abu Ghraib jail in Iraq. I believe many of us see more mundane examples of this every day in the workplace, when good people do the wrong thing because the boss says so. If 65 % of us would be prepared to apply a lethal shock to another human being for $4.50, how many more of us would cheat at work in order to get a bonus or a promotion?

This point is critical for those who are legally responsible for the behaviour of others at work – for example in the financial services industry. An obedience or compliance culture does not necessarily mean an ethical culture. In a compliance culture, people will do the wrong thing if that's what they think is expected of them. Enron is a classic example of this phenomenon. More regulation will simply reinforce the behaviour and authority of those at the top, whether the people at the top are moral or not.

"Conformity is that jailer of freedom and the enemy of growth."

John F. Kennedy

Summary

How does conformity theory help us to decide what's right and find the courage to do it? It teaches us that simply obeying orders leads people to commit appalling crimes. Unless we also base our actions on moral values – on how we think through our actions and empathise with others in the decisions we make – then we risk doing the wrong thing.

"Custom will reconcile people to any atrocity; and fashion will drive them to acquire any custom."

George Bernard Shaw

MoralDNA® – can integrity be tested?

Integrity can be tested. As psychologists Adrian Furnham and John Taylor have demonstrated in *The Dark Side of Behaviour at Work*,[25] we cannot rely on such tests to tell us for sure if someone is a saint or a sinner, even using so-called "lie detectors." But, we can measure our character strengths, weaknesses and level of moral maturity.

This is important in moral decision-making because we ought to be conscious of whether or not we are following the line of least resistance. For example, if we have a weakness in terms of wisdom as a value, then we need to guard against making rash decisions and behaving recklessly or without proper care and consideration. If on the other hand, we show an immature state of moral development by showing a bias towards the Ethic of Obedience, we may struggle to decide what's right when rules are unclear or absent. Integrity testing is useful for judging ethical strengths and weaknesses, not just at an individual level, but also across groups or entire organisations.

In response to the demand for an effective and insightful integrity test, chartered psychologist Pavlos Stamboulides[26] and I began developing the MoralDNA profile in 2008. With the support of Cass Business School, PwC and *The Times* we developed a tool that now measures 13 factors in our MoralDNA. These are the three ethics of Obedience, Care and Reason and the ten moral values of Wisdom, Fairness, Courage, Self-control, Trust, Hope, Love, Honesty, Humility and Excellence. So far over over 80,000 people from over 200 countries have completed the profile.

"The unexamined life is not worth living."

Socrates

The results are striking. As you will see in Chart 1 below, our Ethic of Obedience and our Ethic of Reason are inversely correlated as we mature. This means that the more we develop our Ethic of Reason, the less we will (need to) comply with the Ethic of Obedience. Conformity theory would also suggest that this data supports the hypothesis that the more rules we have, the less people will actually *think* about what's right. These results are also entirely consistent with Kohlberg's Theory of Moral Development.

The other obvious feature is that the Ethic of Care appears to be a constant throughout our lives. Human empathy is widely accepted by neuroscientists to be soft-wired at birth. We are born to love.

As well as age, we can also see another striking result in Chart 2, which shows MoralDNA by gender. Carol Gilligan's insight on the feminine Ethic of Care is clearly demonstrated in our research. Most women prefer to do the right thing because it *feels* right for everyone. Most men, on the other hand, prefer to do the right thing because they *think* it's right. What is also clearly shown in the graph is that females score higher than males

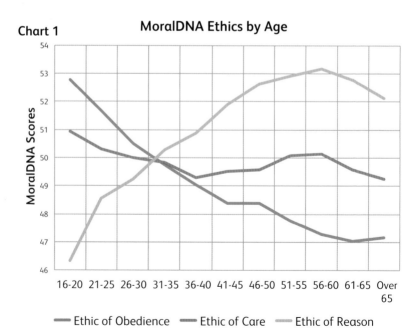

Chart 1

MoralDNA Ethics by Age

Ethic of Obedience — Ethic of Care — Ethic of Reason

Chart 2

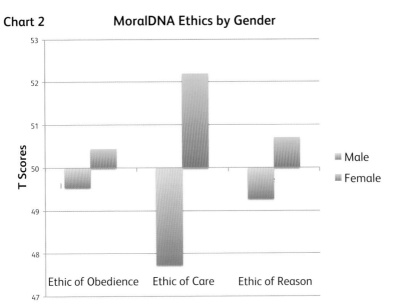

MoralDNA Ethics by Gender

Chart 3

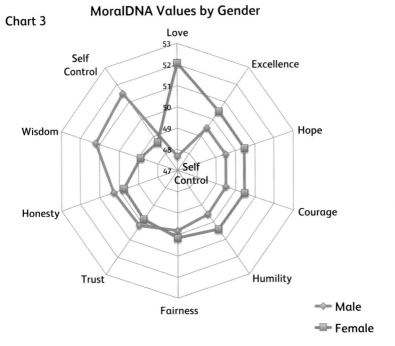

MoralDNA Values by Gender

Chart 4 — MoralDNA Ethics in Life and at Work

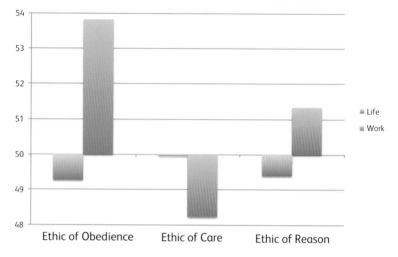

on each of the three ethics factors. Does this mean that women are more ethical than men? We can't draw this conclusion with certainty, but this data suggests that women may be more conscious or mindful of doing the right thing.

When we look at the ten moral values we measure, gender again is a significant variable. In Chart 3, this radar graph should be read like a clock. Beginning at 12 and moving clockwise, female scores are significantly higher than male scores...

So, we can see variations by age and gender. In fact there are significant variations in MoralDNA by nationality, education, religion, politics and occupation. In the workplace our research is now beginning to see what differences there are, if any, in our ethics of Obedience, Care and Reason and our preferences in our personal and professional lives. The results again are striking. In Chart 4 you can clearly see that whilst our score for the Ethic of Obedience increases, our score for the Ethic of Care decreases. We may be more compliant, but we also couldn't care less. Again we see echoes of the Milgram experiment – in a compliant culture, people will prefer to follow orders rather than consider the impact of their actions on others. The challenge for the corporation is to recognise the dangers of this totalitarian, command-and-control, fear-driven culture.

Chart 5

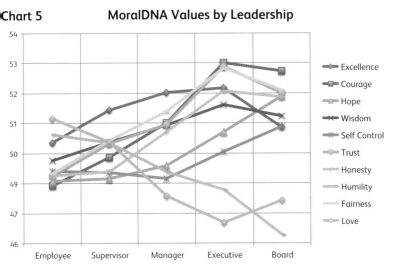

MoralDNA Values by Leadership

Returning finally to our ten moral values, we are also able to see how MoralDNA varies according to organisational status in Chart 5. Whilst we see higher scores on eight of these values, as people become more senior as leaders scores on Humility and Love decrease. Whilst this is not a surprise to many, it might explain why many employees find managers both arrogant and unempathic. Clearly this is in part explained by the gender bias towards male executives at the most senior levels, but this doesn't diminish the ethical challenge for boards and senior executives.

"It is a man's own mind, not his enemy or foe, that lures him to evil ways."

Buddha

Conflict resolution

We have looked at ethics in terms of moral philosophy and in terms of psychology. We can also define ethics as the way we resolve personal "conflicts of desire,"[27] organisational "conflicts of interest" and "conflicts of principle" when values collide. We must also acknowledge that some conflicts are impossible to resolve.

Do I blow the whistle on my boss who's fiddling expenses, even though I risk losing my job after 6 months of unemployment?

Do I keep my promise to see my children in the school play, or close this deal and pay for our holiday with the bonus I'll get?

Do I tell the check out assistant that she's given me too much change?

Do I tell my colleagues husband that his wife is having an affair?

Should I buy organic carrots or the ready meal?

Conflicts of desire

We can define personal ethics as the way we resolve "conflicts of desire," as Plato did in the *Republic*. We are faced with many conflicts every day, although not all conflicts of desire are ethical dilemmas – for example, do I have the strawberry or the chocolate ice cream? But how do we resolve ethical dilemmas? Do we go home to spend time with the kids or stay late at the office to pay for their education? How do we decide?

As we have already mentioned, we can begin by asking the RIGHT questions:

- What are the **Rules**?
- Are we acting with **Integrity**?
- Who is this **Good** for?
- Who could we **Harm**?
- What's the **Truth**?

Faced with the choice of going home to spend time with the kids or staying late at the office to pay for their education, how do these questions help us? In terms of "rules," our employment contract may require us to work the hours required to do our job properly, within legal limits and maximum hours. However, if we've made a promise to our kids that we'll be home early, keeping that commitment could also be regarded as a self-imposed rule. What about our values? Keeping promises might be an important principle, so might relationships based on love, trust and respect. What example do we want to set? Different benefits could result from either course of action. Going home now would clearly benefit the kids today. But staying late to pay for their education might benefit them tomorrow. How about harms? Going home now might mean we can't afford next term's school fees. Staying at the office might mean breaking a promise and causing distress to our children. Finally, are we willing to be open, honest and accountable for your actions, or will we try to find excuses?

In addition to asking the RIGHT questions, when we face any conflict we can also consider the philosophers' "Golden Rule" and "Golden Mean." The Golden Rule says "do as you would be done by" or "how would we feel in their shoes?" This is a powerful perspective because we often forget to consider how someone else might be feeling. The Golden Mean is about "moderation in all things" (mean, in this case, meaning "average" or "middle"). It also has connections with fairness, temperance and balance.

Returning to our dilemma about whether to keep our promise to the kids, the Golden Rule would ask us to consider how we feel when others break their promises to us. The Golden Mean might suggest that we should aim to balance our commitments to work and family. It might also suggest that we aim to balance the time we spend with our children and the time we spend earning the money to support them.

"The 'seven social sins':
Knowledge without character
Science without humanity
Wealth without work
Commerce without morality
Politics without principles
Pleasure without conscience
Worship without self-sacrifice"

Mahatma Gandhi

Conflicts of interest

Just as we have conflicts of desire at a personal level, so we have conflicts of interest at an organisational level. Consider the following list of stakeholders in a typical business:

- shareholders
- bondholders
- creditors
- customers
- directors
- employees
- suppliers
- competitors
- NGOs and other pressure groups
- government and regulators
- local communities
- the environment

How do you think people in business rank them? How do you rank them? This is a question I always ask in workshops, with some interesting results. Audiences are evenly divided in placing the interests of the shareholders, the customers or themselves first. Local communities and the environment often get a mention. I then ask can a business do without any of these stakeholder groups. Of course, the answer is always none. What happens if a business consistently puts the interests of one stakeholder group above all others? Is that sustainable? The answer is, again, no. We, therefore, have to conclude that a successful sustainable business must resolve the interests of all its stakeholder groups fairly. How do we do this? Is there a single formula we can apply to all situations or do we have to consider different answers to different questions? For example, whose interests do we consider when reviewing our environmental policies? How would that look different if we were to consider how we reward our directors? Again, as with personal conflicts of desire, we must consider the RIGHT questions:

- What are the **Rules**?
- Are we acting with **Integrity**?
- Who is this **Good** for?
- Who could we **Harm**?
- What's the **Truth**?

In the UK, all financial services businesses have a legal duty to ensure that they are "treating customers fairly" – for example, when selling pensions. On the surface, this looks like a rule which focuses primarily on the relationship between the retail customer and the company as two parties to a contractual relationship. However, if we consider the RIGHT questions, we begin to see that things are not so simple. The first challenge is to recognise that what looks like a rule is actually a principle. What is fairness? Is it equivalence or what's acceptable? Who decides? The second challenge is to consider that there are other values, some of them also having the force of law. Financial services firms must ensure that they manage their own financial status with prudence by maintaining proper levels of capital and liquidity. What happens when the values of fairness and prudence collide? This we saw with Equitable Life, when for one group of customers to be treated fairly, others claimed they were treated unfairly and the financial integrity of the firm was seriously damaged. Next, which stakeholders' interests should be included in our thinking? Is it just between the customer and the shareholder, or does it involve others? Perhaps an easier question is which stakeholders' interests needn't be considered? In terms of the truth, are we prepared not just to be openly accountable for our actions, but also for the rationale behind our decision? The advantage of being open about why we made a particular decision is that others might disagree with what we think is right, but they will not be able to challenge the integrity of our decision-making process. Finally, what do the Golden Rule and Golden Mean offer us in this scenario? "How would we feel in their shoes?" is a powerful question in this scenario. If we're the financial experts, then we should have a very clear personal idea of what it would mean to treat customers fairly. The Golden Mean might suggest that we avoid making extravagant claims about the performance of a pension fund or investment.

A note on Corporate Sustainability

One of the most important areas of corporate activity today is "Corporate Sustainability." A great deal of effort is expended on process and systems-based approaches to environmental issues, for example, but less attention appears to be paid to the way people in business resolve conflicts of interest in this area. Some critics have argued that corporate sustainability is typically a cynical, outward-facing exercise, when like charity, it should begin at home. Corporate sustainability would, I believe, clearly benefit from a more integrated approach that challenges the individual behaviour of directors and other employees; includes the application of a set of ethical principles that have meaning; clearly evaluates how each stakeholder benefits or is harmed by various policies; and finally exceeds relevant legislation in this area.

"The superior man understands what is right; the inferior man understands what will sell."

Confucius

Conflicts of principle

When values collide, we call these conflicts of principle. Rushworth Kidder and Sheila Bloom at the Institute of Global Ethics have also described these as "right-versus-right" dilemmas.[28] They have described four types:

- **Justice versus Mercy** – We have legal rights and duties, but need also to consider human circumstances and consequences. For example, we might be entitled to enforce repayment of a loan, but we might also want to consider that the borrower is unemployed.

- **Truth versus Loyalty** – This is also known as the whistleblower's dilemma. Do we report a colleague for fiddling expenses and risk becoming unpopular?

- **Individual versus Community** – This acknowledges that we have legitimate self-interest, but when can too much undermine the interests of the wider community? Should directors get paid large bonuses when other employees are being made redundant?

- **Short-term versus Long-term** – This is a key dilemma for business. Do we maximise profits this quarter or do we invest in more call-centre staff to improve customer satisfaction?

  To this list, there is a fifth which is worth identifying because it occurs so frequently:

- **Rules versus Principles** –These two conflict because principles, or values, are general but rules are specific. If we believe in treating customers fairly, what do we do when the regulator says that this means customers must be treated consistently, because consistency is more easily measured than fairness?

When we have to decide what's right, it is vital that we understand how our principles might conflict when we seek guidance from them. In such cases, the Golden Mean is particularly useful – for example, in maintaining balance or harmony between the short and long term. Resolving conflicts of principle is almost by definition a judgement call, as we will see when we examine different scenarios later in the book. There are no hard and fast rules!

"It is our choices… that show what we truly are, far more than our abilities."

J K Rowling

Irresolvable conflicts

Some ethical dilemmas are either impossible to resolve, or we are powerless to do what is right. These often occur in life-and-death situations. I remember reading about a mother and two sons swept out to sea by the Asian tsunami in 2004. She quickly tired and was only able to keep herself and one of her sons afloat. Which son should she try to save and which should she leave to fend for himself? How does a parent make that kind of decision? In the end, I believe she decided to let the eldest and strongest son fend for himself, as he had the best chance of survival. Happily, they all survived.

How do we know that a conflict is irresolvable? Can we tell straight away or should we do our best to resolve it, perhaps with the help of others we trust, before realising there is no right answer, or we're powerless to do what is right? Perhaps the answer is always to do our best to resolve it, but also to accept that we are all human and doing our best is sometimes the only right thing to do.

"Life is like a game of cards. The hand you are dealt is determined; the way you play it is free will."

Jawaharlal Nehru

Summary

Ethics helps us to resolve personal conflicts of desire, organisational conflicts of interest and conflicts of principle when values collide. To do this, we must first understand the nature of the conflict. Where is the conflict? Who does it involve? Then we need to ask and answer the RIGHT questions:

- What are the **Rules?**

- Are we acting with **Integrity**?

- Who is this **Good** for?

- Who could we **Harm**?

- What's the **Truth**?

When we try to resolve conflicts, we must also consider the philosophers' Golden Rule, "How would we feel in their shoes?" and the Golden Mean, "What would be a balanced decision?" If we ask and answer all these questions, people may disagree with what we finally decide is right, but they will find it difficult to challenge the integrity of our decision-making process. We all make mistakes, but this is OK as long as they're honest mistakes.

Applied ethics

In seeking to understand how we decide what's right, we have looked at three ethical consciences, which have evolved over the last 50,000 years. We have also examined more recent psychological and neurological research that helps us to understand our behaviour as human beings. For the final part of our answer to the question, "What is ethics?" we must now look at the range of moral challenges we face in our everyday personal and professional lives. Here we will look at personal morality – for example, how do we decide what's right when a marriage breaks down. We will consider professional and business ethics – for example, how do we resolve the conflict between maximising short-term profit and long-term value in a business. Bioethics and environmental issues are crucial areas because scientific advances appear to be developing quicker than our ability to think about whether it's right – for example, to change life at the genetic level. Finally, we will look at law enforcement and military ethics. Here, too, questions of life and death are critical. How do we decide when it's right for the security services to use force? In this section, we will consider how our emerging approach might be applied in each of these areas. We will then look at some specific scenarios in greater depth later in the book, once we have introduced the complete ethicability framework.

Personal morality

We could argue that every ethical challenge is ultimately a question of personal morality. At work for example, people can argue that they are not personally responsible for their actions because "it's just business" or because they have limited liability; or because they are only one of more than 100,000 employees, so they can pass the buck. The difficulty with this argument is the question, "If I'm not personally responsible, who is?" Can we blame the "system" or do we accept that we all have a part to play in every aspect of our lives – a good part?

So, the first challenge we have to meet is whether it's right to accept personal responsibility for our actions, or do we absolve ourselves of this burden? How do our three levels of conscience help us? Perhaps it's personal only when the rules say it is. On the other hand, if we believe in values, such as courage, fairness, and trust, how can we avoid personal responsibility for our actions? If we consider the consequences of our actions on others in society, then that in itself infers acceptance of some personal responsibility.

So how do we begin to make the RIGHT decision?

- What are the **Rules**?
- Are we acting with **Integrity**?
- Who is this **Good** for?
- Who could we **Harm**?
- What's the **Truth**?

When a marriage breaks down, what do the rules say? In this example, rules don't tell us whether or how to try to save the marriage (unless divorce is forbidden in religious or civil law), they just tell us what provision must be made for the care any children and how any property should be divided.

"Take your life in your own hands, and what happens? A terrible thing: No one to blame."

Erica Jong

How do our values guide us when a marriage is falling apart? Here we must be clear what our values are, together with those of our marriage partner. This is an incredible challenge because the biggest obstacle to making the right decision in terms of values is that our emotions are likely to be drowning out any rational thought processes. Sadness, anger and revenge are unlikely to help us to decide what's right. It's in such circumstances that the old-fashioned virtue of temperance, meaning patience and self-control, assumes such importance. Regrettably, patience and self-discipline are less than popular in a consumerist society. When an old marriage looks worn out, we say let's trade in our old partner for a new model. If, in the end, we still decide that the marriage is doomed, then what values guide our behaviour as we separate? What do fairness, respect and kindness mean in practice?

Finally, how do we maximise the good and minimise the harm when we consider the consequences of our actions? Who are the most important people likely to be affected? Do we decide what's right on our own or can we sit down and discuss it with those concerned? What would be the grown-up thing to do? If we have children, do we put our own happiness before what's best for the kids? Can we distinguish between the two?

The personal moral challenges we face today are increasing dramatically as a result of two powerful forces in our world – at least for those of us in the West. The first is sustained economic growth and prosperity, which now offers almost endless opportunities for overindulgence. As we have already written, our primitive survival instincts keep telling us that we can never have enough food, sex, clothes, gadgets, cars, properties and holidays. We throw away last year's relationships as readily as last season's fashions; and we celebrate celebrities who do all of this bigger and better than us, despite their obvious need for recourse to drugs, alcohol or marriage rehab.

The other factor which we need to face is a general decline in religious beliefs and practices, which have historically moderated these appetites. Perhaps humanity is reaching an adolescent phase in species maturity? We want it, we want it now and who cares about tomorrow? Will we learn to exercise self-control before we die of an overdose of feel-good happiness?

Summary

We need to decide whether everything we do is a question of personal morality, or whether we can blame "the system." Do corporate scandals occur because accounting controls are weak, or because people are greedy? In our personal morality, what are our principles and how important are they? Do we just do anything we like provided it's legal (or if it's illegal, what we can get away with); or do we consider how our behaviour affects others? Do we care more about things and less about other people?

'The line separating good and evil passes not through states, nor between political parties either – but right through every human heart."

Alexander Solzhenitsyn

Professional and business ethics

Professional ethics describe the principles and rules of conduct which govern professions, such as medicine, the law and accountancy. In some instances, such codes of conduct also apply to the personal lives of such professionals: they must not bring the profession into disrepute by, for example, being convicted of a serious criminal offence. This is also becoming more common in corporate codes of ethics. This trend clearly supports the notion that ethics is ultimately personal. Would we need to worry about corporate scandals if it wasn't for personal greed?

Professional codes of conduct generally begin with reference to principles such as "honesty and integrity," "trust" and "fairness." Most, then, catalogue a list of specific rules and regulations presumably for those professionals who are unable, or can't be trusted, to work it out for themselves!

In business, we see a similar pattern. A general statement of principles is followed by even longer lists of dos and don'ts, with some alarming exceptions to general principles. For example, many corporations say that bribery is wrong in principle, but state that you can get permission to make a "facilitation payment" in certain circumstances via a compliance hotline number at head office. The rationale is that in order to do business in certain countries, such payments are a fact of life. What isn't so clear is why they feel compelled to do business in such countries. The alternative is not to have this principle and just be honest about the supremacy of the profit motive.

The first challenge we face, perhaps more so with business than with professional ethics, is the gridlock of increasing regulation as governments try to prevent further corporate scandals. It's clearly not preventing the determined corporate criminal and it saddles everyone else with higher costs. From a psychological perspective, we have already seen that more rules create more rule-breaking behaviours. Nobody wins because nobody is prepared to trust anyone else to do the right thing.

I use the word "gridlock" with good reason. Road traffic is a good analogy for us here. In Europe, we have seen how the roundabout is safer and more efficient than the traffic light at many busy intersections. The traffic light is the equivalent of a rule. It tells you when to stop and go. The roundabout, on the other hand, requires you to exercise personal judgement about when it's safe to join the stream of traffic already on the roundabout. Negotiating a roundabout is about exercising prudence, courage, fairness and self-discipline. Do you think we need more roundabouts and fewer traffic lights at work? What about our lives as a whole?

Business and professional life is an economic activity. In business, whether you're a professional or not, there are many people who need an economic rationale for ethics. Is being good, good for business? The answer is, happily, yes, being good is good for business in the long run. But the converse is also true. Being bad and getting away with it is much more profitable in the short term. So is robbing a bank if you don't get caught!

A number of research teams at universities across the world have tried to analyse what the most successful companies do to set them apart from the rest. What I have done is to identify those actions and behaviours from this research, which we could argue are part of what it means to be ethical. In no less than five major research studies, detailed in Table 3 (see page 78), we can identify certain behaviours, which help to build ethical cultures and lead to sustained business success.

Table 3. Being Good is Good Business

Study	Ethical behaviour
Daniel Goleman, *Leadership That Gets Results,* (Harvard Business Review, Mar 2000)	Goleman outlines 6 leadership styles and demonstrates how empathy (Ethic of Care) is the most effective character trait in 3 of the most successful leadership styles.
James C. Collins, *Good to Great: Why Some Companies Make the Leap… and Others Don't* (HarperBusiness, 2001)	Jim Collins clearly and persuasively argues how moral values such as humility, courage, self-control, hope and passion are at the core of business leaders and culture that excel in the long term.
Bill George and Peter Sims, *True North: Discover Your Authentic Leadership* (Jossey Bass, 2007)	A great collection of stories about successful business leaders who are humble, passionate, human and authentic.
James C. Collins, *How the Mighty Fall: And Why Some Companies Never Give In* (Random House Business, 2009)	In contrast with *Good to Great*, Jim Collins shows how the moral vices of ego, greed, self-denial and fear destroy businesses.
Raj Sisodia, Jag Sheth and David Wolfe, *Firms of Endearment*, Pearson FT Press, 2014	Firms of Endearment profiles 73 businesses including IKEA, Southwest Airlines and Unilever, which are built on love, passion and a purpose to serve others - and yet have achieved five times the stock market returns of the S&P500 over 14 years!

The most striking research is Jim Collins's *Good to Great*, where, out of 1,435 companies, he identified the 11 best performing. These companies averaged cumulative returns of no less than 6.9 times the stock market average for at least 15 years. What were common to each of these corporate cultures were the good old-fashioned virtues of personal humility, intense resolve (courage) and discipline (self-control).

Another issue we must consider is that we are currently measuring success in business with accounting conventions and standards which now account for less than 50 % of the value of the average corporation. Baruch Lev is the Philip Bardes Professor of Accounting and Finance at New York University, Stern School of Business. He and others have measured the relationship between profit and stock return since the mid-1960s.[29] In the last 40 years, the relationship between average increases in profits and average increases in stock market value has declined from a near perfect correlation, to about 50 %. In other words, if a company's profits increase by 10 % today, we can only expect to see a 5 % increase in its stock market value. So what accounts for the rest, if it isn't purely profit? The answer includes things like brand, reputation and intellectual capital, which together is sometimes called "goodwill" – what an interesting word for the philosopher! The "bottom line" is no longer the bottom line. So why do we continue to run our businesses as if it was? Why do we focus on profit rather than value? Why do we care more about this quarter's results and care less about risking our goodwill in order to make the numbers?

Having established that our professional, working lives can be more successful and sustainable if we behave virtuously, can the same be said if we just do what is legal, or what creates the maximum economic benefit for key stakeholders or a combination of the three? The answer surely has

"A business that makes nothing but money is a poor business."

Henry Ford

to be a combination of shared values; wealth creation for all stakeholders; and action within a compliant legal framework. So, how do the RIGHT questions help us resolve the conflict between short-term profits and long-term value creation?

Acting lawfully is essential both to short-term profits and to long-term value creation. However, does too much regulation create cultures where the maxim is "as long as it's legal, it's right," simply because there are so many rules limiting the opportunity for profit? A perfect example of this is how businesses exploit tax loopholes. Tax evasion is illegal, but by definition, tax avoidance is not. Therefore, businesses are constantly seeking opportunities to minimise tax. This can dramatically increase cash profits. However, if a company says it aims to "act in the public interest" it may be legal to minimise tax payments, but is it right?

A principled approach to the conflict between short-term profitability and long-term value creation will inevitably aim to balance the two. We have already identified discipline and intense resolve as key virtues for the "Good to Great" business, but wisdom is also important here. It requires us to generate sufficient profits to pay the bills and to keep us going as a viable business. For example, Citigroup, the US banking conglomerate, has had its share of ethical challenges in the last few years. In September 2004, Citigroup CEO Chuck Prince said, "We have to have the moral compass to deliver those profits and growth responsibly and honestly. Citigroup's culture must be synonymous with integrity."[30] In other words, it's not just how much money we make in business, it's how we make it that counts.

In terms of benefits and harms to stakeholders, again we need balance and fairness. As we have already seen, balance is an important concept in resolving conflicts of interest. We need to consider both the Golden Mean and the Golden Rule, that is, "moderation in all things," and "do as you would be done by." What this implies in practical terms is that if we

"Hire character. Train skill."

Peter Schutz

maximise short-term profits, we are by definition not seeking an optimum level of profits. When we maximise short-term profits, we are more likely to do things which put fragile long-term assets like reputation, at risk. This approach may mean great news for shareholders who are seeking a dividend income, but bad news if you're in most of the other stakeholders' shoes: employees earn less; customers pay more; suppliers get less; long-term shareholders risk long-term value; regulators get suspicious and so on. In summary, we could argue that balancing the needs of stakeholders in business is an exercise in wisdom, fairness and self-control. We're back to those moral values again!

*"If I only had a little humility,
I would be perfect."*

Ted Turner

Summary

If personal morality is challenging, professional and business ethics are infinitely more demanding because of the complexities of having so many other people's interests represented in the workplace. If we are to avoid gridlock at work we need fewer traffic lights (less regulation) and more roundabouts (more shared moral values). Studies, such as Jim Collins's *Good to Great*, have demonstrated that good businesses become great businesses because, like the driver on the roundabout, they navigate using moral values such as courage and self-control. Like the courteous driver, they also demonstrate personal humility. Being good is good for business.

Bioethics and the environment

Bioethics and environmental issues are concerned with fundamental issues of life, death and existence. Science is advancing faster than our ability to decide what to do with new technologies and whether we should develop them. Whilst pollution and other obvious environmental issues have received a great deal of attention over recent history, the debates around bioethics are the most challenging. There are fundamental and seemingly irreconcilable differences in philosophy between all those concerned. Scientists focus on the good created, for example, in curing inherited genetic conditions through manipulating DNA. Business seeks to exploit these new technologies for profit. Religious leaders say that their faiths allow no compromise when it comes to issues of life and death, for example with abortion and euthanasia. There are politicians and the press who argue over these issues for votes or for circulation. Finally, there are the rest of us who have to get on with living and dying in this brave new world that's being recreated around us.

Whilst we can barely scratch the surface of the bioethics challenge in this book, we should recognise that these questions have to be addressed sooner rather than later. Bioethics already touches every part of our lives. How do we decide what's right when a relative is dying a painful death from cancer? If we work as a professional or in business in this area, how do we know we're acting ethically? Do we agree with our religious leaders on these matters? If we have no faith, what principles guide our thinking? Can the RIGHT questions help us here?

So, what are the rules? Well, there are now thousands of rules governing bioethics, but these vary hugely depending on the jurisdiction. In the US, for example, prior to 2009 the impact of political lobbying by evangelical Christian groups had resulted in a ban on the federal funding of embryonic stem cell research. Following President Barak Obama's intervention[31] this ban was lifted, allowing the US to come into line with certain other European countries where such research is taking place, although still strictly regulated. Regulations also vary widely when it comes to many other bioethics issues, including assisted suicide; sperm and egg donation; payment for blood and organ transplants; spiritual drug use; transsexuality; and the use or denial of life-support systems.

There's no doubt we need to have some agreed rules in this area otherwise we could easily do something that could have a global impact. Perhaps we should first develop a shared understanding about which values we should derive our rules from, and then consider what would benefit mankind as a species in the long run.

Let's start by thinking about some of the values which might help. Wisdom, for example, suggests that whatever we do in this area, we must understand the risks, as well as the rewards, for humanity. For example, we now have the power not only to destroy life on earth through nuclear fission, but also by genetic mutation. We are already developing genetically engineered anti-bacterial killer viruses. What if one of these mutated naturally into a deadly new pathogen? Self-control, meaning temperance and patience, also suggests caution. On the other hand, the values of love and kindness might suggest we do everything in our power to save a dying relative or friend, but like other moral values, love should be universal. Would it be right to threaten the lives of others with the release of a "doomsday" virus, in order to save the life of a loved one? What do your values suggest?

What does our Social Conscience say? What would benefit mankind in the long run? Remember, our ethos here is that what is right is what maximises benefit for the greatest number. But what do we mean by "benefit" and what do we mean by the "greatest number"? Does benefit mean feel-good happiness and pleasure, or value-based happiness and the good

"The saddest aspect of life right now is that science gathers knowledge faster than society gathers wisdom."

Isaac Asimov

life? Do we proceed with age-defying technologies or do we accept the inevitability of our mortality and focus on dignity and care for the elderly? Then, what do we mean by the greatest number? Does this mean those who can afford to buy advanced biotechnologies or those who can vote for such advances; or does this have to concern everyone on the planet? What do you think would benefit man in the long run?

Summary

Bioethics and our environmental impact on the entire planetary ecosystem present us with the greatest moral challenges. These issues are of vital importance to every human being today, right now. They already impact our daily lives. For the last 20 years, every part of our global ecosystem has shown signs of malaise as a result of environmental pollution. We can no longer simply leave it to the "experts" because different experts in science, religion, politics and economics have conflicting interests and perspectives. The questions we need to ask and answer are fundamental to our existence. I believe that philosophy can help us to decide what's right. I'm not certain we are smart enough to tackle these challenges yet, but I hope we are smart enough to recognise that we need to develop brave new thinking before we build our brave new world. In the meantime, perhaps patience really is a virtue.

"Without ethics, everything happens as if we were all five billion passengers on a big machine and nobody is driving the machine. And it's going faster and faster, but we don't know where."

Jacques-Yves Cousteau

Law enforcement and military ethics

Whilst the threat of global warfare between nations has receded, we face new challenges to our security. The enemy is now within. Whether it's armed robbery, money-laundering, drug-trafficking or terrorism, the threats to our security are real, they're personal, and they could be living next door. Set-piece battles between standing armies are being replaced by conflicts of ideology. In the past, we could identify an armed enemy soldier in uniform. Today, the enemy might be someone sending a text message. We cannot imprison greed. We cannot shoot dead an idea.

The challenge we face today with crime and violence at any level is an ethical one. The thief who steals our identity has a philosophy of naked self-interest and greed. The habitual Saturday night binge drinker lives a life that lacks any real meaning. The terrorist with a bomb wants to impose his philosophy by force. Law enforcement agencies and the military are, therefore, not only facing a challenge of physical security, which must still be countered by reasonable force, but they are also facing a challenge to their moral integrity.

Two recent examples clearly demonstrate this dilemma. As Britain was preparing to send its forces to Iraq in 2003, military chiefs had serious concerns about the legality of the war and General Sir Mike Jackson, was quoted to have said, "I spent a good deal of time recently in the Balkans making sure Milosevic was put behind bars. I have no intention of ending up in the next cell to him in the Hague."[32] Not only were there concerns about the legality of war, but also concerns about the morality of war. For example, one of the long-established moral arguments for a just war is that war must be the absolutely last resort. There are equally clear and long-established principles about the treatment of prisoners which many feel are threatened by our primitive limbic reaction to the threats we face.

In the second example, the British police are also asking questions about their role in society. In the 2005 Richard Dimbleby Lecture, the Metropolitan Police Commissioner Sir Ian Blair asked the simple question, "What sort of police service do you want?" He pointedly asked this question after the UK parliament reduced to 28 days the British government's proposal for 90-day detention-without-trial for terrorist suspects. The police had supported the 90-day proposal.

In order to answer both Sir Ian Blair's question and General Sir Mike Jackson's concerns, we need to ask and answer a bigger question, "What sort of society do we want?" This again becomes a philosophical question. Do we want to live in a society which is even more highly regulated, with more security cameras and with more police having greater powers? Do we want a society which seeks to maximise feel-good happiness for the voting majority? Or do we want a society where values and principles mean something? Could we have the best of all these approaches?

A detailed consideration of these questions is beyond the scope of this book. However, a recent policing story offers hope that building a society and a culture based also on moral values, can work. In Britain, a Lincolnshire policeman, Gary Brown, has started a "Knight School" where more than 100 children and young people have been taught a medieval code of chivalry, emphasising courtesy, manners and community work. Since its inception, youth crime has halved in the town. Such has been the impact of this approach that Gary tells me he receives over a thousand e-mails daily, from all over the world. With this project, we can see the Ethic of Care at work in the chivalric code with its emphasis on courtesy, manners and respect.

Perhaps we can also recognise what's best in terms of law enforcement and military ethics when the worst happens. After 9/11 and the London bombings on 7 July 2005, what was striking was the instinctive reaction of the police, the emergency services and ordinary people caught up in these disasters. Perhaps fear and intolerance can only be defeated by the virtues of courage, kindness and the generosity we might wish to remember and celebrate from those shocking attacks.

KNIGHT SCHOOL

Summary

Law enforcement agencies and the military are facing challenges perhaps greater than any weapons of mass destruction. The enemy is within. It is now the viruses of greed, violence and intolerance that threaten our communities and these cannot be arrested, imprisoned or shot. We need to decide what kind of society we want before our police and soldiers can decide how best to do their duty. We can argue that force is sometimes our only option, but ultimately violence, crime and intolerance can only be defeated by values such as courage, justice and patience.

*"Leadership is a potent combination of strategy and character.
But if you must be without one,
be without the strategy"*

General Norman Schwarzkopf

What is ethics? – Summary

Ethics is the study of moral philosophy, which helps us to decide what's right and act accordingly. We have evolved three broad approaches to this question. The first is the Ethic of Obedience, which means that what's right is simply obeying rules for reward or fear of punishment. The second is the Ethic of Care, based around empathy and love, and enables us to work out who benefits or is harmed by our actions. The third is the Ethic of Reason, incorporating wisdom, justice and self-control. We can see how as children we first learn right from wrong by being told. Then as we grow into adolescents, we think about the consequences of our actions on others. Finally, we mature as moral grown-ups and learn wisdom and self-control as the adult alternative to obedience.

Integrity is the principle which defines all our moral values. We have integrity if we live our lives according to a shared set of moral values. If, however, we act against those values, then we lose our integrity. We call this hypocrisy. If we doubt the integrity of others without just cause, we call this cynicism. Our collective, social integrity is based on the Ethic of Care. Our personal integrity is based on the Ethic of Reason.

Our moral philosophies have now given us a framework to ask the RIGHT questions:

- What are the **Rules**?
- Are we acting with **Integrity**?
- Who is this **Good** for?
- Who could we **Harm**?
- What's the **Truth**?

We can also think of ethics as the way we resolve conflicts of desire in our personal lives, conflicts of interest in our working lives, and conflicts of principle when values collide. To help us resolve these conflicts, we can use the philosopher's Golden Rule, "How would we feel in their shoes?" and the Golden Mean, "What would be fair and reasonable?"

Psychology helps us to understand the games people play in order to influence other people's behaviour. We need to understand that economic game theory cannot explain what is fair; our sense of justice is not driven simply by a cool, calculating cost-benefit analysis. If we want a rule-based culture, we can act as parents and tell others what to do. Unfortunately, if we do other people begin to act as children and stop taking responsibility for their actions. We have also seen that within a rule-based, authoritarian culture, 63 % of ordinary people will be prepared to kill another human being simply because they're told to do so.

If we want to maximise happiness for the greatest number, doesn't that sound great? But feel-good happiness is a mirage. We run the risk of becoming addicted to feel-good pleasures in life and our morality is determined by the philosophy of the cancer cell – growth at all costs, even if it kills us. Our focus becomes more work, more money, a bigger house, a better car, more holidays, but less time for others and less time for relationships. The wheel has come full circle. The new science of happiness is simply proving what philosophers knew thousands of years ago, that enduring happiness is values-based. The good life is a life lived according to moral values that guide the way we live for and with others.

When we apply ethics to any aspect of life, we can try to blame "the system" when things go wrong, but ultimately we are all responsible for our individual and collective behaviour. At work, we face significant conflicts of interest which constantly need resolving. But if we succeed in making good decisions and doing the right thing, the rewards are exceptional. Being good is good business.

Finally, we face two immense threats to our civilisation. Science now enables us to change the very nature of life on our planet. The challenge in bioethics and the global environment is to develop a new science of thinking to help us decide what's right or face extinction. We also face new enemies within. The viruses of greed, violence and intolerance pose another lethal threat to our civilisation, whether it's the corporate fraudster or the terrorist bomber. We need to decide what sort of society we want before we decide how the policeman and the soldier should protect it.

Ethics is the new frontier.

"Every person must decide whether he will walk in the light of creative altruism or the darkness of destructive selfishness. This is the judgment. Life's most persistent and urgent question is, what are you doing for others?"

Dr. Martin Luther King, Jr.

Ethicability

How to decide what's right and find the courage to do it

"Here is the beginning of philosophy: a recognition of the conflicts between men, a search for their cause, a condemnation of mere opinion, and the discovery of a standard of judgment."

Epictetus

Ethicability:
How to decide what's right and find the courage to do it

Having explored the nature of ethics, we are now ready to understand and practise using the ethicability framework with real-world ethical dilemmas and scenarios. Ethicability is not a rigid process. For example, when working with senior executives who are paid to make quick, instinctive decisions, they are encouraged to offer these immediately. One of these could be right, but which one? Then we can begin using the ethicability framework.

"The world we have created is a product of our thinking; it cannot be changed without changing our thinking."

Albert Einstein

ethicability®

Preparation
Time out!
How do we feel?
Who's involved?
What are the facts?
What sort of dilemma is this?
What are our intentions?
What are our options?
Have we thought creatively?

Decide what's RIGHT
What are the **Rules**?
Are we acting with **Integrity**?
Who is this **Good** for?
Who could we **Harm**?
What's the **Truth**?

Testing our decision
How would we feel in their shoes?
What would be fair and reasonable?
What would be the adult thing to do?
What would build trust and respect?
What would stand the test of time?
Have we the courage to do what's right?
What can we learn from this dilemma?

As you can see, ethicability consists of 20 short questions arranged in three stages. Each question is there for a very good reason as together they incorporate the critical insights we have learned from moral philosophers and social psychologists. Together, these questions help us to decide what's right. By asking and answering these questions we can also become confident that we have made our decision with integrity and from this confidence we can find the courage we need to do the right thing.

At the core of ethicability are the RIGHT questions we have already used. Remember, if you need to make a quick decision, make the RIGHT decision.

As we explore the ethicability framework, let's think about the following dilemma, which will help us to understand why we need to ask these questions. This scenario looks at the tensions between our personal and professional lives. It's about truth and divided loyalties.

> **Jane is a senior human resources executive within your company. She has just been told in strict confidence that one of the business units is being closed down. Given the difficult trading conditions faced by the organisation as a whole, the opportunities for new employment within the business for the 20 employees concerned, are zero. Jane's best friend, Helen, works in this unit. Helen is a single mother with a two-year-old daughter and is the executive assistant to the business unit's managing director. Jane and Helen trust each other completely when it comes to sharing confidences. Helen had phoned Jane earlier to say that she was planning to complete the purchase of a new and larger apartment that afternoon. The company is not yet in a position, nor is it yet legally obliged, to make any official announcement on possible job losses.**

Should Jane respect her professional duty of confidentiality and say nothing; or should she do "what's right" for her friend and tell her, or at least drop her a hint?

Let's now think about this dilemma as we introduce ethicability.

Preparation

Time out!

The first step is to take "time out" to deal with the problem or dilemma. Decide who needs to be involved and get them together in a room away from distractions, particularly mobile phones and e-mail devices. You should give yourself at least an hour for your discussions. More complex issues may take two or three hour-long sessions with breaks in between to gather more facts and opinions from relevant parties, groups, stakeholders or their representatives.

> In our first scenario, Jane does not have much time. She cannot involve Helen in the discussion without, in effect, telling her or dropping a hint. She would probably not want to involve her boss, who would almost certainly remind her of her professional duty. That could, of course, resolve the dilemma immediately, but experience suggests that most people would perhaps talk to a trusted colleague instead. When running this popular scenario in workshops, I've asked delegates to say what they think most people would instinctively do, and not surprisingly, most say that most people would at least drop a hint.

"When you encounter difficulties and contradictions, do not try to break them, but bend them with gentleness and time."

Saint Francis de Sales

How do we feel?

We will often feel a range of emotions when confronted with an ethical dilemma: anger, fear, frustration, stress, concern, guilt and anguish. Any such emotions should be articulated, acknowledged, and then set to one side as we begin our deliberations. Ethicability recognises the power of emotions, but also reminds us that deciding what's right is a rational and reasonable process between two emotional stages. At the outset, we acknowledge our perhaps negative emotions and set them aside. At the conclusion, we need to build on the strength that reasoning provides and build new, more positive emotions around courage, confidence and conviction.

> Jane would clearly be feeling concern for Helen, her daughter and their friendship if she did nothing. She would also be worried about her job if she said anything that breached her duty of confidentiality – provided this was discovered.

"Get mad, then get over it."

Colin Powell

Who's involved?

We easily forget that when we face ethical dilemmas, we are not really dealing with abstract arguments; we are dealing with real people and real lives. It is vital that we ask and answer the question, "Who's involved?" although with quite complex scenarios, the question we should be asking is, "Who's not involved?" For example, a business might wish to consider all the stakeholders we listed in the section "Conflicts of Interest." In an ideal world, you would try to gather representatives of all affected parties involved in the discussion, but if that isn't possible, ask someone in the room to role-play any absent but critical party.

> The obvious key players in our drama are Jane, Helen and Helen's daughter. But who else is involved, particularly if Jane did decide to drop a hint and was somehow found out? What if the business unit was involved in a market sensitive area and any news of closure affected the share price? What if the case somehow went to an employment tribunal and the press reported it in some negative way? Within the business, we must therefore consider the other 19 employees in the doomed business unit, any other employees, the shareholders, customers, lawyers, government agencies and the press.

"We are afraid to care too much, for fear that the other person does not care at all."

Eleanor Roosevelt

What are the facts?

We will often feel a range of emotions when confronted with an ethical dilemma. When we rush to a decision, the risk of missing a vital piece of information is immense. Ethicability requires us to gather all information relevant to our dilemma. If time makes it difficult to gather all these facts and opinions, note any assumptions you may make and be prepared to reconsider your decision if any contradictory evidence comes to light at a later date.

> Jane is clearly concerned that Helen is about to commit herself to a larger mortgage and then find herself without a job. Jane instinctively begins to think the worst. However, we are jumping to a conclusion that Helen could be unemployed for some time. How likely is that? She could find a new job quite quickly. She will also receive a severance package which will buy her more time. She could even end up being better off!

"You know, the very powerful and the very stupid have one thing in common. They don't alter their views to fit the facts, they alter the facts to fit their views, which can be uncomfortable if you happen to be one of the facts that needs altering."

Doctor Who, the BBC

What sort of dilemma is this?

Conflicts of principle happen when values collide. We looked earlier at "right-versus-right" dilemmas described by Rushworth Kidder and Sheila Bloom at the Institute of Global Ethics. It is important therefore to ask which conflicts of principle exist within a particular scenario. These are: Justice versus Mercy; Truth versus Loyalty; Individual versus Community; Short-term versus Long-term; and Rules versus Principles. Let's look at these in our scenario:

Justice versus Mercy is about applying rules but also considering the very real human consequences of doing so. Jane is clearly concerned that whilst Justice demands that she must maintain confidentiality, Mercy is suggesting that she do something to help her best friend and her friend's daughter. However, we can also argue that every other human being who could be adversely affected by this situation and any action we might take should also be considered. Truth versus Loyalty is quite complex here as both truth and loyalty are operating at several levels: the principle of honesty might suggest that here confidentiality should be broken; but also that Jane must be prepared to act openly with her decision. With loyalty, we have a clear conflict between personal and professional loyalties. Individual versus Community is an obvious conflict: does Jane act in her own and Helen's best individual interests or does Jane do what's best for the wider community of stakeholders? Finally, we have Rules versus Principles. Rules here are clear; Jane must maintain her duty of confidentiality both as an employee and as an HR professional. But how does Jane square her personal and professional principles? These might also demand that she respects her professional duty to treat all employees fairly, but what about the principles of care, trust and loyalty to her friend?

What are our intentions?

Intent is an important concept in deciding what's right. Having good intentions is not in itself a sufficient justification for what we do, but it is a useful question to ask. With ethicability, our intention is to do what's RIGHT. We must consider the rules, the principles that guide our actions and the consequences of our actions for all involved. Although these perspectives may themselves conflict, we must be clear about what we decide to do and why. If we are then prepared to be openly accountable for our actions, then we have done our best to make our decision with integrity. That must, ultimately, be our intention.

Jane's intentions here must be to do what's right both personally and professionally and to reconcile her conflict of loyalties. In short, she must be certain she has made the right decision and be accountable for it. If this is the case, how then do we consider the option of "dropping a hint"?

"Remember, people will judge you by your actions, not your intentions. You may have a heart of gold – but so does a hard-boiled egg."

Unknown

What are our options?

In many dilemmas we face, the obvious choice is what logicians call a binary decision. Do we do something or nothing – that is, do we do A or B. The more complex the scenario, the less likely this is to be the case. As we consider each of the ethicability questions, possible solutions can be voiced at any time. Write them all down, no matter how bizarre they sound. The right decision isn't always the most obvious or the most palatable.

> On the face of it, Jane is faced with a binary decision: keep a professional confidence, or tell Helen something sufficient for her to consider whether she should complete her apartment purchase. If we decide to say something, then should we be direct or just drop a hint? The next stage is where we consider creative alternatives.

"Choices are the hinges of destiny."

Edwin Markham

Have we thought creatively?

Creative decision-making is fun, especially with a group. The ethicability framework is designed to get us looking at any dilemma from 360 degree, multi-dimensional perspectives. A method that has proved extremely effective is to ask everyone to think of options quietly, without discussion, for about three minutes. Then everyone has to share their insights followed by a lively debate. At the end, we will be left not only with two or three options, but also the beginnings of a shared understanding of their relative strengths and weaknesses.

When running this scenario for real, there have been some entertaining options, including placing a higher bid for Helen's apartment! Once the fun has died down, the most frequent options proposed are: to do nothing; to say something directly; to drop a hint; or to escalate the issue to the boss.

"Perhaps imagination is only intelligence having fun."

George Scialabba

Decide what's RIGHT

We are now ready to evaluate our options against the RIGHT questions representing the Ethic of Obedience, the Ethic of Care, the Ethic of Reason, all our moral values and the truth and accountability test.

What are the **Rules**?

When we speak of rules, we mean any relevant laws, regulations, rules codes, contracts and anything else that states legal rights and duties. If we find a rule that specifically tells us what or what not to do, then this is the beginning and the end of the process. However, rules, like principles may conflict, especially between legal jurisdictions; or they might not tell us clearly what to do or may not address the issue we face. If in doubt, this is the time to check with a lawyer, a compliance officer or the company secretary. However, just because something is not illegal, doesn't mean it is right.

> **In the dilemma faced by Jane, the rules are clear. She has a contractual duty as an employee to maintain confidentiality in such matters. She may also have a professional duty to do the same through membership of a professional HR institute. There are also likely to be specific legal processes in place which any court or tribunal might have to consider if the case went to a hearing – for example, if the other 19 employees found they had been unfairly treated by not getting the same information at the same time as Helen.**

"If one is not capable of knowing the law and living within the rules of it, he is never capable of being a free man."

John Locke

Are we acting with **Integrity?**

In order to answer this question, we must know what our moral values are. It sounds obvious, but you'd be amazed at the number of people and organisations who have never articulated their values or principles. Regrettably, I sometimes work with organisations that have clearly defined principles, but when a profitable deal is at risk, they admit they will breach the principles and do the deal if the lawyers say it's not illegal. One senior US attorney admitted to me that his organisation's business principles were merely window dressing for PR purposes. They would always do business if it was both profitable and legal. If in any doubt about what these principles should be, we could do worse than begin with the ten moral values described earlier – wisdom, fairness, courage, self-control, trust, hope, love, honesty, humility and excellence.

Jane is probably thinking of how her personal values as a friend should guide her decision. She feels that loyalty, trust and concern for her friend's welfare are paramount. However, we should also remember that moral values are universal insofar that these same values should guide how she acts in relation to everyone involved. This is where humility, fairness, courage and self-control are needed and this is where the Ethic of Reason and the Ethic of Care overlap.

"On a personal level, everyone must answer the following question: What is my highest aspiration? The answer might be wealth, fame, knowledge, popularity or integrity. But if integrity is secondary to any of the alternatives, it will be sacrificed in situations in which a choice must be made. Such situations will inevitably occur in every person's life."

Murphy Smith

Who is this **Good** for?

Asking and answering this question is the first stage in thinking of the consequences of our actions on others. What we do is to take each of our options and ask who would benefit and how. This means we have to consider every relevant or interested party listed in answer to the question, "Who's involved?"

> If Jane decides to do nothing, we could argue that no one actually benefits because all she is doing is maintaining the status quo. However, if Jane does say something to Helen either directly or by dropping a subtle hint, then clearly Helen and her daughter are likely to benefit. Jane, too, may benefit if Helen regards her actions as a sign of an even greater friendship. If Jane's actions are discovered by the other 19 employees, they too may benefit either by seizing the same opportunity to start preparations for redundancy, or begin preparing a claim for unfair dismissal.

"Never let a man imagine that he can pursue a good end by evil means, without sinning against his own soul. The evil effect on himself is certain."

Robert Southey

Who could we **Harm?**

Thinking about who could be harmed is often more important than thinking who benefits. This is where the values of wisdom, fairness, self-control and respect for others must counter the philosophy of "every man for himself and devil take the hindmost." Do remember, however, that you can have too much of any moral value, and that some harm to someone is virtually inevitable. What we must do when we have worked out the answer to this question is to see whether the goods outweigh the harms. For the utilitarian, this would be a sufficient test on its own, but remember that the RIGHT questions consider the merits of each of our moral philosophies.

> **If Jane decides to do nothing, then Helen and her daughter might be harmed in the short term. Much depends on how much Helen gets as a severance package, how long it takes her to get a new job, and whether it pays more or less than this one. If Jane says something and this remains secret, then the only harm might be to her conscience or to her soul. However, this is why the truth question is vital. We must ask who could be harmed if Jane says something and this is discovered. Jane's job and career is harmed; other employees' interests may be harmed; if the business closure is market-sensitive information, then shareholders, customers and many others could be harmed. In short, the potential harm in saying something and being accountable significantly outweighs any possible benefit.**

"No one ought to harm another in his life, health, liberty or possessions."

John Locke

What's the **Truth?**

When children do something wrong, they quickly learn that if they can deny it or hide any evidence then they are unlikely to be punished. This lesson is difficult to unlearn. This is why we must always ask ourselves the question, are we being open, honest and accountable for our actions? We should also go further and ask, are we willing to be open, honest and accountable for the reasons behind our decision and our actions? If we can, then the clarity of conscience and the confidence this brings will help us to find the courage to do the right thing.

> In ethicability workshops, most people say that most people would drop a hint in this scenario. This is exactly what happened in the real-life incident on which this scenario is based. "Jane" dropped a hint to "Helen" in a bar at lunchtime and she was overhead by one of the other 19 employees in the business unit. Back at the office, the employee challenged senior management about possible closure on the basis of this overheard conversation. "Jane" was summoned to the HR director's office, admitted her error, and was immediately suspended pending a full disciplinary investigation. She was later dismissed for gross misconduct and her professional career in HR was finished.

"There is no god higher than truth."

Mahatma Gandhi

Testing our decision

At this point, you should have made a decision about what's right. This must now be tested against each of the following tests. It is my experience that most decisions will pass almost all these tests once you have reached this part of the ethicability framework. Then again, we all make mistakes, so run through these final tests to build the confidence and courage you may need to turn decision into action.

How would we feel in their shoes?

This is the Golden Rule, which is often stated as "do as you would be done by." This is how we resolve conflicts of interest as we consider everyone else's perspective as if it was our own and ask how we would feel about the decision that is being made.

Let's assume that Jane decides after all to maintain her duty of confidentiality and do nothing. How would you feel about this if you were Helen and her best friend? Would you think that Jane had done the right thing? On the other hand, what if she had dropped a hint and then, as happened, not only been fired, but destroyed her professional career?

"Tzu-kung asked, 'Is there a single word which can be a guide to conduct throughout one's life?' The Master said, 'It is perhaps the word "shu." Do not impose on others what you yourself do not desire."

Confucius

What would be fair and reasonable?

Here we have the Golden Mean, or simply stated, "moderation in all things." This is how we resolve conflicts of desire and conflicts of principle by avoiding extremes. The opposite of a virtue is a vice; too much of a virtue is also a vice.

> If Jane decides that she must be guided by personal loyalty to her friend above all others, we could see this as too much personal loyalty. Another outcome that might be seen as fair and reasonable could be to discuss this with her boss, a middle way between saying something and doing nothing.

"Our moral theorists seem never content with the normal. Why must it always be a contest between fornication, obesity and laziness, and celibacy, fasting and hard labor?"

Martin H. Fischer

What would be the adult thing to do?

This question reminds us to check that we have approached our dilemma from a rational, adult perspective, rather than as a purely rule-based parent-to-child transaction, or as a frivolous, self-indulgent child-to-child interaction. This, however, is not a hard and fast rule, as some dilemmas might require a firm reminder or application of clear rules.

If Jane decides to drop a hint rather than be open and honest about her actions is this a grown-up or childish action? Is doing our duty an adult or childish thing to do? Is doing what's right even though it may harm us or a loved one, a childish or a grown-up thing to do?

"It takes courage to grow up and become who you really are."

e e cummings

What would build trust and respect?

Trust is a synonym for faith. Together with self-control, they are two of our ten key values and are important in building a community that has integrity. An organisation without trust and respect is unlikely to be very moral for very long. We need to test whether or not our decision reflects these principles.

> If Jane says something to Helen, trust and respect between them might increase, but at the risk of trust and respect being damaged both for Jane and, perhaps, for the company as a whole. If Jane keeps her confidences, then trust and respect may diminish for Helen, but it may not. We could argue that a true friend might want you to do the right thing.

"If you lie, people will distrust you; if you tell the truth, people will dislike you."

Oscar Wilde

What would stand the test of time?

One of the greatest challenges we face today is that we tend to live for today. "I want it; I want it now; and I don't care about tomorrow," is the mantra of homo economicus. This egoistic philosophy pervades not just our economic behaviour but also our relationships one with another at work and at home. This means that as we face moral dilemmas, we will go for the quick fix which works today, but could fail tomorrow because we haven't thought it through.

> **If Jane says something to Helen, her focus is today. What she is not considering is the long-term impact on her own situation if she is found out, which could mean the end of her professional career in HR.**

"And in today already walks tomorrow."

Samuel Taylor Coleridge

Have we the courage to do what's right?

As ethicability evolved, it became clear to me that making the right decision wasn't very difficult if you asked all the right questions. The greatest difficulty is not in deciding what's right, but in finding the courage to do it. However, it became clear that when working with people facing real challenges, the ethicability framework removed fear of the unknown and created confidence that a decision made had been made together and had been made with integrity.

If Jane says something to Helen, it is partly because she fears for Helen's immediate well-being and perhaps their friendship. Ethicability offers her the chance to see beyond these immediate threats and to put them into a rational perspective where doing the right thing is actually counter-intuitive for most of us.

"A coward is a hero with a wife, kids and a mortgage."

Marvin Kitman

"Courage is resistance to fear, mastery of fear – not absence of fear."

Mark Twain

"The most effective way to do it, is to do it."

Amelia Earhart

What can we learn from this dilemma?

When we finally make or agree on our decision about what's right, it's worth thinking about how the dilemma arose in the first place. What should we now change about the way we live and work to reduce or remove the chance of similar issues arising in the future? One of the most powerful things we can do is to articulate and affirm our principles both individually and collectively. In my work with businesses, for example, this has been a consistent consequence of the work we have done together.

> **Let's assume that Jane decided the right thing to do was to keep matters confidential. In due course and at the appropriate time, she can sit down with Helen and tell her what happened and why she made the decision she made. Jane still has a job in HR and is well placed to help Helen find a new position. What they can both learn from this is that sometimes we have to trust our friends to do what they think is right because that's what friendship is about.**

"Learning is a treasure that will follow its owner everywhere."
Chinese Proverb

We have now explored the ethicability decision-making framework with a conflict of truth and loyalties faced by Jane. What was your instinctive decision when you first read the scenario and would you now do anything differently? What did you learn?

Now we have seen how ethicability works, there are four further scenarios for you to consider. There is a deliberate mix of dilemmas combining a variety of applied ethics, including personal, professional, business and medical. After describing each dilemma, please use the framework to decide what you would do. If you get stuck, then I have printed some tips at the foot of the next page for each scenario. I will not share my decision in each case, as the point of the exercise is for you to learn how to decide what's right for yourself.

Dilemma 1 – Tax avoidance and social responsibility

Your company is a global organisation based in the US with operations in more than 60 countries. It has made the following commitment to social responsibility. "We aspire to be recognised as a company dedicated to the communities we serve, taking a lead role everywhere we operate and make a positive difference where we work and live."

Your corporate tax experts advise you to adopt a tax avoidance scheme in an Asian country, where you have a significant operation employing 10,000 people locally. The scheme is based on an unintended tax loop-hole in the latest Finance Act that will reduce your corporate tax bill by at least $20m a year. Your organisation makes profits of US $10bn a year.

Tax avoidance is, by definition, legal, but would it be right to act on this advice? Would you act differently if you had no local operations in the country concerned?

Hints and tips

This is a popular scenario in ethicability workshops and clearly focuses on some key dilemmas. The obvious conflict appears to be the stated commitment in principle to social responsibility wherever the company operates, and the legal duty of executives at US corporations to maximise shareholder profits. What are the rules? There's nothing to say you can't adopt the scheme. How do our principles guide us? Integrity suggests we shouldn't adopt the scheme. Are we acting with integrity? Adopting the scheme benefits shareholders, but harms local stakeholder interests. However, if you adopt the scheme and the government makes a fuss, there could be a significant reputational risk, which would then harm shareholders. Did you consider not only the relationship with the local community, but also with the local Finance Ministry? What sort of relationship do you want with the tax authorities? If you take the advice, you might be subject to retaliation and a thorough tax investigation. In ethicability workshops, most groups decide not to act on the tax avoidance advice.

Dilemma 2 – Friendship and fraud

Your best friend works in a company where you are head of internal audit. Your wives are best friends, too. You are all very distressed as three months ago his wife was diagnosed with a cancer for which there is no effective treatment currently available within your country. However, he tells you that he has found out about a pioneering new treatment that harvests and grows the body's own T-cells to attack the tumour. The only problem is that a complete course of the therapy will cost more than $500,000, which he cannot afford, even if he sold their home.

Today, you have spotted what appears to be a complex fraud on a $3bn government contract, which appears to have been perpetrated by your friend. The sum embezzled is $350,000, but the evidence linking him to the fraud is circumstantial. Do you proceed with a full investigation, confront your friend informally, or let it go?

Hints and tips

This is a more acute version of the Jane and Helen dilemma we worked through earlier. However, your best friend's wife is facing a terminal illness, not just financial embarrassment. How do you feel? Feelings will play a big part in this dilemma, not just for you, but for your wife, too. Do you discuss it with her? What are the facts? The evidence is circumstantial, given what's at stake for your friend's wife. How would she react if she found out that her husband was being investigated for fraud? What are the rules? You really have no option but to take some action. Are we acting with integrity? Whose principles matter? If you take action, what good would it do now? The crime may have already been committed. If you act now, it's clear that not only will you destroy any hope of treatment; the impact of an investigation will make it difficult for your friend to care for his wife. What about truth and accountability? No one else has noticed the fraud and no one yet knows that you've spotted it. If anything gets out, you're probably in the clear. But if you begin an investigation, everyone will know what you've done. Whatever you decide, you will need great courage to do what's right. For many people this is an irresolvable dilemma.

Dilemma 3 – Too old and ugly?

You are a non-executive director of a leading, publicly listed cosmetics firm. Your company is being sued for gender discrimination by a former sales executive who claims she was fired by her boss, the sales director, for being "too old and ugly" for the job. The case has already been widely reported in the press. Your lawyers have interviewed all the other members of the sales team and have confirmed that your sales director has a very aggressive management style, but find no specific evidence of gender discrimination in this case. Some members of the sales team have indicated that they think their former colleague is "trying it on" for a substantial settlement. Attempts at mediation have failed. Your lawyers have advised you that your only defence is to argue that there was no gender discrimination as the sales director treats everyone equally badly, including male colleagues. Another employer has recently used a similar defence and won.

The board has to decide whether it should defend the case using this argument, even though your published business principles say that, "Respect is a core value for our firm," and "People are our most important asset". Or should you settle out of court for whatever it takes, even though you suspect the claimant is "trying it on"?

Hints and tips

This is based on a real case from the US in April 2004. The first issue here is that we cannot be absolutely sure of the facts. We do not know if he said she was "too old and ugly" or not. However, the fact that her boss has a very aggressive management style is not disputed and forms the basis for your defence. Is this a problem? What sort of dilemma is this? It has elements of every one of our five conflicts of principle. Who's involved? Everyone, because it is partly an issue of reputation, win or lose. What are our intentions? Not only to resolve this case, but to deal with the issue of why this "very aggressive" behaviour is tolerated, given your business principles. What are the rules? They conflict. Directors have a legal duty to protect shareholders assets, but employers have a general duty of care to employees. Are we acting with integrity? This is a real issue, whatever the outcome of the case. When you consider harms and benefits, there are three possible outcomes: defend the case and win; defend the case and lose; or settle out of court. Which would be the best and worst outcomes? In terms of honesty and accountability, if you go to trial, there will be a lot of dirty washing. If you're still unsure what you would do, think about your options against each of the seven other tests before you make a final decision. In ethicability workshops, most groups decide to attempt an out-of-court settlement, together with a serious review of the company's culture.

Dilemma 4 – Medical ethics and healthcare rationing

Your mother is suffering a severe personality disorder and your local doctor has arranged for a consultant psychiatrist to visit her at home. The purpose of the visit is to certify and commit her as an in-patient at a psychiatric hospital in another region, which has a bed available. The psychiatrist needs a second doctor's signature in order to certify her and a junior doctor is despatched from your local surgery to your home to do just that. When the junior doctor arrives, he examines the patient and discusses her symptoms with the psychiatrist. You are shocked to discover that your mother is actually not sufficiently ill to be certified, but this is the only way she can get treated. The junior doctor is reluctant to agree to this breach of professional medical ethics.

As your mother's carer, what do you feel is the right thing to do: support the psychiatrist who says this is the only way she can get treated, or support the junior doctor and risk her condition deteriorating further?

Hints and tips

This is based on a real dilemma discussed at a general practitioners' conference. On the face of it, there seems to be a strong argument to agree with the psychiatrist and have your mother committed so that she can be treated – the end justifies the means. However, this would mean a breach of medical ethics and of your mother's human rights. How do we feel? Emotional. What are the facts? There's an unspoken issue here about healthcare funding and rules. Have we thought creatively? You could try to appeal to the regional authority to have the rules changed so that your mother can be treated out of the region without being certified. What are the rules? She should not be certified. Are we acting with integrity? Whose principles and which principles is critical here. Who would benefit and how? It looks like your mother would benefit most. Who would be harmed? The professional integrity of all involved. Would you wish your mother to be treated by a psychiatrist who is prepared to breach professional ethics? The honesty and accountability test is failed if she is certified. In ethicability workshops, most groups decide that medical ethics are paramount, but would take legal action to see that treatment was authorised without the need for your mother to be certified.

Living a good life, building a better world

Living a good life, building a better world

I hope that this book has given you some practical insights into what we mean by ethics and why we do what we do. Ethicability has been designed and tested in the real world to help you make tough decisions in your life – whether they are professional or personal. In our ever-stressful world, we face a multitude of challenging decisions. But by following ethicability's no-nonsense framework, I am confident that each and every one of us can make the right decision – a good decision – when we ask and answer these questions:

Preparation
Time out!
How do we feel?
Who's involved?
What are the facts?
What sort of dilemma is this?
What are our intentions?
What are our options?
Have we thought creatively?

Decide what's RIGHT
What are the Rules?
Are we acting with Integrity?
Who is this Good for?
Who could we Harm?
What's the Truth?

Testing our decision
How would we feel in their shoes?
What would be fair and reasonable?
What would be the adult thing to do?
What would build trust and respect?
What would stand the test of time?
Have we the courage to do what's right?
What can we learn from this dilemma?

"I WANT IT,
I WANT IT NOW,
and I don't care about
tomorrow"

Some contemporary philosophers such as Alisdair MacIntyre[33] and Stanley Hauerwas[34] have argued that any discussion of ethics in terms of pure reason is a futile and pointless argument. For such thinkers, ethics is only meaningful within the context of a moral community and the moral leadership within that community. The challenge we face today is that there is no global consensus about what is right because there is no single and coherent global moral community. So, we have to do the best we can wherever we can. We can all accept responsibility for our own actions. We can decide what's right as members of a family, as a circle of friends and as neighbours. At work, we can turn the rhetoric of organisational principles into a meaningful reality for deciding what's right – it certainly works for those businesses that have survived and prospered in challenging times.

We should be clear about our philosophy in life. Do we do anything we like as long as it's legal? Do we try to build societies which maximise their own economic well-being? Or do we build a global civilisation based on universally accepted principles? Will we continue to behave as spoilt moral infants or will we grow up? Do we continue to blame others, or should we search inside ourselves for the enemy within?

Ethicability has evolved not only to help us decide what's right, but also as a critical approach to help us find the courage to do it. If you had to choose one of these philosophies in preference to the others, what would it be and what would it mean? By asking and answering these questions, can you find the courage to live your life accordingly?

Ethicability asks a final question "What we can learn from this dilemma?" What have you learned from reading this book? Whoever we are and whatever we do, we are all individually responsible for our own decisions and actions. What we do and how we do it also has a direct impact on our family, friends, work colleagues and all those we meet in our daily lives.

And, for those of us who are responsible for the lives or livelihoods of others, we need to consider whether our influence and our leadership will be a force for good or ill.

We must decide what's right and find the courage to do it.

The enemy is within!

Notes

Footnotes

1   Presidential advisor James Carville, the 1992 Clinton campaign.

2   Forms and Limits of Utilitarianism, David Lyons, 1965.

3   *The New York Times Magazine*, September 13, 1970.

4   "Boycott threat to stores selling 'sexy' clothes for six-year-olds"
        Evening Standard (London), Sept. 21, 2005.

5   *The Sex Education Show, Stop Pimping Our Kids*, Channel 4, first shown Tuesday 19th April, 2011.

6   *Oxford Dictionary of English*, Second Edition Revised, Oxford University Press, 2005.

7   *The Corporation*, Joel Bakan, Simon and Schuster, 2004.

8   *Essays in Moral Development I-II*, Lawrence Kohlberg, Harper and Row, 1981, 1984.

9   Thomas Hobbes, *Leviathan*, 1651.

10   *In a Different Voice: Psychological Theory and Women's Development*, Carol Gilligan, Harvard University Press, 1982.

11   *After Virtue*, Alasdair MacIntyre, Gerald Duckworth & Co. Ltd., 1981.

12   Michael Kirkwood CMG, Director, UKFI, interviewed by the author.

13   Search result from google.com on 6th October, 2011.

14   *Integrity in Practice*, Christopher Jamison and Roger Steare, Financial Services Skills Council, 2003.

15   *The Secrets of Happiness*, Steven Reiss, Psychology Today, Jan/Feb 2001.

16   *Happiness – Lessons from a New Science*, Richard Layard, Penguin Allen Lane, 2005.

17   *Games People Play*: The Psychology of Human Relations, 1964 (1978 reprint, Grove Press).

18   Adapted from Transactional Analysis at wikipedia.org.

19   *How (Un)ethical Are You?*, Banaji, Bazerman and Clough, *Harvard Business Review*, December 2003.

20   Güth, Werner, Schmittberger and Schwarze, *An Experimental Analysis of Ultimatum Bargaining, Journal of Economic Behavior and Organization*, 3:4 (December 1982).

21   *The Neural Basis of Altruistic Punishment*, Dominique, de Quervain, Fischbacher, Treyer, Schellhammer, Schnyder, Buck and Fehrl, Science, 27 August 2004.

22   *Journal of Abnormal and Social Psychology*, Milgram, 1963.

23   *The Perils of Obedience*, Milgram, 1974.

24   *Journal of Applied Social Psychology*, Blass, 1999.

25   *The Dark Side of Behaviour at Work*, Adrian Furnham and John Taylor, Palgrave Macmillan, 2004.

26   psycholate.com

27   *A Short History of Ethics*, Alasdair MacIntyre, Routledge, 2nd Edition, 1998.

28   *Ethical fitness in today's business environment*, Rushworth Kidder and Sheila Bloom from *Business Ethics*, ed. Moon and Bonny, Economist Books, 2001.

29   *Taxable Income, Future Earnings, and Equity Values*, B. Lev and D. Nissim, *The Accounting Review*, October 2004.

30   *Can Chuck Prince Clean Up Citi?* Mara Der Hovanesian, Paul Dwyer, Stanley Reed, Bloomberg, September, 2004.

31   US Government Executive Order 13505, March 2009.

32   *Revealed: The Rush to War*, Richard Norton-Taylor, *The Guardian*, 23rd February, 2005.

33   *After Virtue*, Alasdair MacIntyre, Gerald Duckworth & Co. Ltd., 1981.

34   *A Community of Character: Towards a Constructive Christian Social Ethic*, Stanley Hauerwas, University of Notre Dame Press, 1981.

Index

Further reading

Games People Play: The Psychology of Human Relationships, Eric Berne, Penguin Books, 1970

After Virtue, Alasdair MacIntyre, Gerald Duckworth & Co. Ltd.,

1981 *Essays in Moral Development I-II*, Lawrence Kohlberg, Harper and Row, 1981, 1984.

A Short History of Ethics, Alasdair MacIntyre, Routledge, 2nd Edition, 1998

A Better Way to Think About Business, Robert Solomon, Oxford, 1999

Leadership that Gets Results, Daniel Goleman, HBR, 2000

The Secrets of Happiness, Steven Reiss, Psychology Today, Jan/Feb 2001

Business Ethics, Economist Books, 2001

Good to Great, Jim Collins, Random House, 2001

Moral Capitalism, Stephen Young, Berrett-Koehler, 2003

Authentic Happiness, Martin Seligman, Nicholas Brearley Publishing, 2003

Integrity in Practice, Christopher Jamison and Roger Steare, Financial Services Skills Council, 2003

The Corporation, Joel Bakan, Free Press, 2004

The Dark Side of Behaviour at Work, Adrian Furnham and John Taylor, Palgrave Macmillan, 2004

The Man Who Shocked the World: The Life and Legacy of Stanley Milgram, Thomas Blass, Basic Books, 2004

The CEO and the Monk, Cattell, Moore and Rifkin, Wiley, 2004

Toward a Theory of High Performance, Julia Kirby, Harvard Business Review, July-August 2005

True North, Bill George, David Gergen and Peter Sims, Jossey Bass, 2007

How the Mighty Fall, Jim Collins, Random House Business, 2009 *Inspiring Leadership*, Jonathan Perks, Fisher King Publishing, 2010 *Trust, The Behavioural Challenge*, pwc.com, 2010

Ethical Breakdowns, Max Bazerman and Ann Tenbrunsel, Harvard Business Review, April 2011

Firms of Endearment, Raj Sisodia, Jag Sheth and David Wolfe, Pearson FT Press, 2014

Primed to Perform, Neil Doshi and Lindsay McGregor, HarperBusiness, 2015

Thanks to…

This book is dedicated to my Dad, Peter Steare.

Dad, as with most dads, taught me right from wrong. His "day job" was construction, but he was also a part-time Methodist preacher and, after he retired, an Anglican priest. On Sundays as children we would travel from chapel to chapel, where in some villages our family would double the size of the congregation! But what were most memorable were my Dad's sermons. His message was always delivered with passion and absolute conviction. He died of cancer in 2003, having been cared for to the end by my devoted Mum. My memory of him is one of "tough love." He was a man of integrity and moral conviction, but he was also "a lovely man," as my wife, Jane, put it. He showed me that doing right could be tough, but was the key to a good life. When he became an Anglican priest, he gained a distinction in his ethics examination and I hope he approves of this work, dedicated to his memory.

There are three other people I would like to thank for their influence and support in my work.

I first met David Wenman in 1985. He was a partner in O'Connor Securities, a Chicago-based futures trading firm. He was setting up a London office and asked me to help him recruit some people for it. We lost touch after a few years, until he read a half-page profile in the Financial Times on work I was doing as a career coach. We had lunch and he said he wanted to invest in my new business because he believed in me and my principles. David has steadfastly supported me and the business over some very challenging times as ethicability has evolved. David has been a great benefactor and friend. I am eternally grateful for his faith in me and this work.

Christopher Jamison, OSB, is Abbot of the Benedictine monastery at Worth, which was featured as The Monastery on BBC TWO in 2005. I first met Christopher at Ashridge Management College in late 1993, where we had both enrolled in a programme called "Action Learning for Chief Executives." At the time, Christopher had recently been appointed headmaster of Worth School and I had just been appointed CEO of a financial services recruitment business. Together with David Simpson,

Paul Barrow and moderator David Pearce, we worked together on business and personal issues in the business equivalent of "group therapy." In 2002, we both decided to do something about the lack of spirituality in contemporary work and founded "The Soul Gym" at Worth Abbey. The Soul Gym provides senior executives with the space to reflect on and "work out" what's right. Our first assignment together was to co-author a paper commissioned by the UK Financial Services Authority called "Integrity in Practice," and much of the core philosophy at the heart of ethicability was developed with Christopher, who has a master's degree in theology and philosophy. Christopher is a great thinker, writer and speaker and remains a close friend and mentor. Without him, ethicability would not exist.

Christopher delivered a memorable best man's speech at my wedding in 2003. In it he said, "I'm privileged to count Jane as a friend." Indeed, Jane is the best friend anyone could want. She is, without a doubt, the most remarkable human being I have ever met. She has suffered great tragedy in her life, yet she works hard as a reflexologist and healer. Jane has an acute sense of "what's right" and she keeps me on the straight and narrow in terms of both the big and little issues. For instance, we were finishing lunch one Sunday at a restaurant. I asked for the bill, only to find that we had not been charged for two glasses of wine we had ordered. Like many, my initial reaction was to relish this rare moment of good fortune until Jane leaned over and asked, "So remind me what it is you do?" To have someone like Jane not only as a friend, but as your wife, is a rare privilege and gift.

My aim has been to build ethicability on sound philosophical and behavioural foundations. It has also greatly benefited from the contributions and feedback of literally thousands of senior executives and learning professionals over the last 9 years, not least psychologist Pavlos Stamboulides and our associates listed at ethicability.org. Thank you so much for your advice, feedback and above all, your friendship.

I am deeply grateful to Ned Hoste at 2h for superb design and project management; to Jacky Fitt for her efficient and sensitive editing; to Tim Bulmer for his wonderful illustrations; Alison Farrell for her proofreading and to Sarah Hilton for indexing.

Ethicability learning resources

As of January 2019, it has been adopted as the core content for leadership and culture change programmes for over 600,000 employees in businesses with a combined market capitalization of over £300bn.

This book has been designed as a stand-alone learning resource for the individual. But at the organisational level, people will get the greatest benefit by using the book to support an interactive workshop or learning event lasting from between three hours to three days for groups of between 12 and 40.

Typically, participants will complete an individual MoralDNA profile and some light pre-reading so they come to the event with some insights. The organisation also benefits from some objective analysis and reporting on its MoralDNA.

The design of the event will include the core content of ethicability so that participants not only understand and practise the decisioning framework with relevant dilemmas, but also the moral theory behind it. Longer workshops can include a more complex business simulation, together with wider empathic leadership skills and exercises.

Corporately branded editions of *ethicability*

Ethicability has been designed for corporate branding by adding your company logo, a message from your CEO on the inside front cover, a statement of your own business principles and your logo on the ethicability card. This offers a powerful message of commitment to integrity not just for your employees, but also for customers and other stakeholders.

Advisory services and speaking engagements

In addition to the design and delivery of ethicability workshops, Professor Roger Steare is a trusted advisor, critical friend and disruptive thinker to business leaders. He is also in high demand as a conference, offsite and after-dinner speaker. As the creator of the ethicability framework, Roger is uniquely placed to offer powerful and creative insights to the moral challenges facing people and organisations today.

For further information on all these resources, please contact Roger Steare at:

Roger@TheCorporatePhilosopher.org

TheCorporatePhilosopher.org
MoralDNA.org